PROTECT YOUR PEACE

ALSO BY TRENT SHELTON

The Greatest You: Face Reality, Release Negativity,
and Live Your Purpose

Straight Up: Honest, Unfiltered, As-Real-As-I-Can-Put-It
Advice for Life's Biggest Challenges

***

PROTECT YOUR PEACE

NINE UNAPOLOGETIC PRINCIPLES
FOR THRIVING IN A CHAOTIC WORLD

TRENT SHELTON

HAY HOUSE, INC.
Carlsbad, California • New York City
London • Sydney • New Delhi

Published in the United States by: Hay House, Inc.: www.hayhouse
.com® • *Published in Australia by:* Hay House Australia Pty. Ltd.: www
.hayhouse.com.au • *Published in the United Kingdom by:* Hay House
UK, Ltd.: www.hayhouse.co.uk • *Published in India by:* Hay House Publishers India: www.hayhouse.co.in

Cover design: Micah Kandros • *Interior design:* Nick C. Welch

**Cataloging-in-Publication Data is on file at the
Library of Congress**

Hardcover ISBN: 978-1-4019-7316-2
Autographed edition ISBN: 978-1-4019-7775-7
E-book ISBN: 978-1-4019-7317-9

10 9 8 7 6 5 4 3 2 1
1st edition, January 2024

Printed in the United States of America

This product uses papers sourced from responsibly managed forests.
For more information, see www.hayhouse.com.

SUSTAINABLE
FORESTRY
INITIATIVE

Certified Chain of Custody
Promoting Sustainable Forestry
www.forests.org
SFI-01268

SFI label applies to the text stock

*This book is dedicated to my mother,
Aqua Shelton. Thank you for showing
me the importance of peace.
You will live on forever. I love you.
This book is also dedicated to my father,
George Shelton. Thank you for instilling
the values in me that have now
inspired the world. I love you, Dad.*

CONTENTS

ACKNOWLEDGMENTS

Maria, Tristan, Maya, and Marlee, you are my world. Thank you for always supporting me, loving me, and being my peace.

Shout-out to my bro Matthew Merchant for helping me bring this book to life. I appreciate your dedication and help throughout this process.

Brenda, thank you for everything. RehabTime wouldn't be able to reach the world without you.

INTRODUCTION

Constant Battle

Before we get started, I want to take a second to say thank you. Thank you for taking ownership over your life. Thank you for embarking on a journey the majority of people may never go on. Many people talk about change. Many of them project the image of change. But the reality is, according to some recent research, only 8 percent actually put in the work to *create change*.

The goal is not for you to start this book—anyone can do that. The goal is for you to *finish* the book, be in that 8 percent, become what I call an "8 percenter," and understand what *protecting your peace* is all about.

If I could pass on one thing to my kids and loved ones, that's what it would be: how to create and *protect their peace*. I don't mean me protecting their peace *for* them. I'm talking about showing them how protecting my peace changed *my* life, in the hope that it will inspire them to create their own unique formula. The intention of this book is similar. I haven't created a strict how-to manual that tells you exactly what to do to protect *your* peace. Instead, I'm going to share my process, and what I have gained from creating it, to help you jump-start a process of your own. Along the way, you'll come to understand what I mean when I talk about peace—and why protecting yours is the most important thing you can do.

THE BATTLE FOR YOUR PEACE

I need you to understand something. What we will discuss in the following chapters is a matter of life and death. I'm not talking about physical death—at least, not right away—but a different kind. You see, losing your peace will lead to an internal death. The death of your dreams and your goals. The death of your best, most fulfilled self.

The battle going on for your peace is a silent one—and there have been too many people who have already lost these silent battles. In a world full of posts, filters, and Photoshop, it's not hard to guess why many of us feel so let down when we aren't perfect. When trying to be perfect (a losing game 100 percent of the time), we fail to talk about our silent battles. This can lead to serious depression, one of the major thieves of our peace. In 2021, 48,183 people in the United States alone took their life by suicide.[1]

I dedicated my life to helping people in 2009. The catalyst was when one of my best friends, my college roommate, Anthony, took his own life. At the time, I felt I could have done more. I felt like I wasn't there enough. It was gut-wrenching to be so close to someone but then realize how far away I was from understanding what he was going through. Although it was devastating, Anthony's life was not lost in vain. At that moment, I redefined my mission, which led me to many callings that I couldn't have imagined before. It led me away from the career I'd hoped to have as a pro football player. It led me to create my nonprofit organization RehabTime, a platform that has allowed me to speak from my heart and develop ideas that have resonated with people around the world. It has led me to a place where I can inspire people to recognize their greatness and become the best version of themselves. And it's led me to create this book for you.

I know God has allowed me to have certain experiences in my life, so that I can be a vessel to assist others in realigning themselves on the path toward peace. I've learned to identify common themes that I see in people who are losing their peace so that I can help them on this path. And the path starts with disconnecting from whatever may be stealing your peace to begin with. I'm guessing that you're familiar with many of these thieves yourself. Maybe you're in a silent war with one or even several of them right now. That's okay. I've been there. Just because you've had a few bad chapters, that doesn't mean your story can't end well. *Those chapters don't have to define your life.* In fact, they can be used to *refine* your life, depending on your perspective and willingness to heal.

If y'all are with me and ready to boost your life with the key ingredient that so many overlook daily, I need you to repeat this mantra with me out loud:

I. Declare. War!

War against anything and everything that is taking away from my . . .

P-E-A-C-E

This simple five-letter word is the key that unlocks ultimate satisfaction and true happiness. *Internal wealth.*

A PRESCRIPTION FOR PEACE

What comes to mind when you think of the greatest wealth in the world? Dollar signs? Certain celebrities? The blue check mark on your socials? Mansions? Extra commas and zeros in your bank account? If so, don't feel bad. Many of us associate wealth with these *things*. In fact, that's how I thought for many years of my life. I believe we are programmed to think this way. It's part of the age we live in. Isn't it ironic that although there is a heavy cost that goes along with each of the items listed above, the inner peace that you cannot see or hold in the palm of your hand is what is truly priceless? *Peace does not depend on everything going on around you. It depends on what is going on inside you.*

Look up the word *peace* in the dictionary, and you'll see it defined something like this:

1.   Freedom from disturbance; tranquility.

2.   A state or period in which there is no war or a war has ended.

The second definition brings me back to an important point. There *is* a constant battle, both internal and external, that we all face for our peace every day. In today's world, where technology is advancing by the day and there is never a shortage of distractions, the enemy just gets stronger and stronger. One of my goals in this book is to help you understand where the battle lines are. I want you to understand your own worth so you'll know just how much you have to fight for.

I have heard before that some things in life are simple but not easy. For example, going for a walk in nature is simple for many of us. But distractions like scrolling on our phone might make it not so easy to find the time to go

THERE IS A CONSTANT BATTLE, BOTH INTERNAL AND EXTERNAL, THAT WE ALL FACE FOR OUR PEACE EVERY DAY.

for that walk. Simple, not easy. Like many aspects of life, when I think of peace, it seems *simple* in its nature—yet *not easy* to attain or sustain. It must be protected at all costs.

So, in this book, I want to offer you my own prescription for peace.

My personal prescription—we'll call it the Protect Your Peace Process—involves nine principles, divided into three sections. The first section, Protect Your Energy, discusses the power of boundaries, the importance of disconnecting from negative distractions, and knowing your own worth. The second section, Protect Your Mind, teaches you how to trust your vision, guard your focus, and shift your perspective. In the final section, Protect Your Soul, we'll talk about how you can create happiness, align internally, and live in fulfillment. At the end of each chapter, you'll find a Protect Your Peace Practice to help you put the ideas to use right away. I hope you keep note of your responses and share them on your social if you're inspired. Be sure to tag me @TrentShelton so I can see how you're doing!

A CRITICAL MESSAGE

Before we dive in, I have to share another foundational piece that led me to this moment with you. In 2015, life was the definition of bittersweet for me. My career as a speaker and coach was taking off, the videos I made were spreading, doors were opening, and people were starting to discover me. I embarked on a 32-city tour. My team handled all the logistics, rather than using Ticketmaster, Live Nation, or anyone like that. We sold out every U.S. city and were fortunate enough to book several shows outside the United States.

But then I burned out. I had very little peace. Everything was great externally, but internally I was defeated. I hate to say it, but these gifts and blessings God had given me began to feel like a burden. I felt like I was in prison within my purpose. That was on me, though. I had yet to understand boundaries, or the other principles of peace that we are going to dive into in this book.

In San Francisco there was one memorable night when I felt empty but determined to fill others up. I remember praying backstage, "God, please just use me. I don't know what I have left in me, but please just use me how You want to." Despite feeling drained, I was able to get onstage and deliver. After my talk I went around smiling and taking pictures with attendees, still feeling empty inside. I found the back door of the venue, which led to a smoky alleyway, like in the movies. It was dark and I thought I was alone, so I let myself break down. "What's going on?!" I cried out. *This is supposed to be better; I am supposed to feel better.*

Just then I looked up and saw what appeared to be an unhoused man listening to me.

To make myself feel better, I thought, *let me bless this man.* I reached into my pocket for a hundred-dollar bill and held it out. "No, I don't need that," he said. "Don't feel sorry for me. I actually feel sorry for you. I see your name and face on the billboard and how you are the guy everyone is here to see. I'm looking at you right now and it seems like you have a lot missing from your life. It seems like you have everything that means nothing. It may look like I have nothing, but I still have everything. That's because I have peace. I have peace in my life that's unconditional, and my spirit can always identify a soul that's missing what it needs most."

I hopped in my rental car and drove down to the waterfront, which was not far away from the venue. The salt in the air and the sea breeze on my face was deeply refreshing as I looked out over the bay and just prayed. I simply asked God to fill me up with peace. This was the moment where the words *protect your peace* were birthed into my soul and became a standard of how I would live my life from then on.

Looking back and piecing all of this together, I now realize that God not only helped me on stage that night. He also gave me the gift of a breaking point, and he gave me a messenger in a form that I did not expect, which led me to seek what I now see as the single most important thing. My pursuit of peace officially started in that moment. Since then it has taken me through many ups and downs. Each step along the way has continued to emphasize that no matter how much you seem to have externally, it will never define or sustain your happiness. That comes from realizing what is truly important in life. That comes from your *peace*. The time is now to recognize and protect it!

What I'm sharing with you in these pages is my journey. I hope it will inspire you to go on your own journey, which might look different from mine. I am here to give you everything I have. But like I have always said . . .

It all starts with you!

PART I

PROTECT YOUR ENERGY

PRINCIPLE 1

SET BOUNDARIES

*Life is too short to spend another day
at war with yourself.*

— RITU GHATOUREY

Welcome to the first part of our journey together. I'm glad you're here. Over the next three chapters, we will dive deep into the importance of *protecting your energy*.

Energy is everything. It should be protected by any means. It's our most precious resource, so it deserves the utmost respect. This is vital to your life, because the more you tolerate from this world, the more you separate from your inner peace. Think of protecting your energy as a safeguard for your personal well-being. Imagine it as drawing a protective circle around yourself. In this circle, your energy isn't wasted but used wisely on what truly matters to you. This is the kind of life worth living, isn't it? Each time you protect your energy, you send a powerful message: "I value myself." By the end of Part I, my sincere hope is that you establish firm boundaries that cannot be compromised, recognize the importance of disconnecting as needed, and feel confident in understanding your own worth. Now let's get to work on the first step: setting these boundaries.

Let's be real: the world comes at us fast these days. Demands and requests pour in left and right, from our work and our communities, from our friends and families, or from complete strangers. These demands often come in with no regard to whether or not they're good for *you*— chances are, they're from people who want your time, your money, your energy, and ultimately your *peace*. The more you let these requests and demands in, the more you give yourself away. Keep doing this and then one day— *boom*. You're done. You've given all yourself away, and you don't know how to get yourself back.

There was a time in my life when I was spread too thin. Trying to take care of situations over here, people over there, and issues somewhere in between. Trying to be everything everyone wanted me to be. But my life gained so much clarity when I began to feel the power in setting boundaries. When I claimed the right to say, "Nah, I ain't feelin' that." Felt the power in standing up for myself and telling people what I wasn't going to tolerate. I put boundaries in place so that I could live my best life. Some people took offense. Some people saw this as me being cold, distant, or unhelpful. That's fine with me. Like I said, I developed this skill so that I could live my best life, and if me living my best life offends you, then I don't need you around. Sorry / not sorry!

Let's get one thing out the way: I am going to challenge you. Straight up. If this was easy, we wouldn't be having this conversation. You're going to need some thick skin. If you've already got that, great. If not, don't worry—I'll help you add it to your bag as well. But you're going to have to hear some tough truths. There's no other way through.

FLIP THE SCRIPT

Here's the first of those tough truths: many of us are professional people-pleasers, or "Triple Ps," as I like to call them. Triple Ps are worried about what other people think and easily manipulated by the perception that they're letting someone down. But when we seek to please others above even ourselves, it almost always leads to being drained, burned out, or feeling stuck. We give it all away to others and leave nothing in the tank for ourselves.

How do I know? I've been there. I believe I have one of the biggest hearts out there, and before I figured out how to create boundaries for myself—before I figured out how to protect my own peace—it used to get me in a lot of trouble. Not anymore! I refuse. Does this mean I've got it all figured out now? No. I catch myself slipping sometimes. But after some practice, I know what to watch for and how to recall my boundaries rather than just pleasing others.

How did I do it? First of all, it was a *must* for me to grow my emotional intelligence, and it was a *must* for me to figure out how to not only create but *stand firm on* my boundaries. As I like to say: *I love helping people with their problems—until their problems become my problems.* That's a boundary I've created, and I stand on it.

I believe many of us struggle with setting boundaries because we worry too much about what other people think. Worry and guilt are first cousins—worry is the reason why people don't set boundaries; guilt is the reason people don't stand firm on them. Our ideas about self-worth more often come from how others see us than from how we see ourselves. Sad but true. If we're programmed this way, but we decide to look at what we want (instead of what others want for us), it opens us up to feeling we're letting people down and failing to live up to their expectations for us. We start to feel we have to choose what *they* want over what *we* want in order to avoid that painful guilty feeling.

Do you battle with these negative feelings? Do you worry that you're letting people down? Do you feel guilty when you can't show up for someone when they ask you to because you are choosing to show up for *you*?

If so, you have come to the right place. Our first order of business in the Protect Your Peace Process is to flip the script on all that. When you feel worry or guilt, it's not all the way bad because it means that you really care. You have a big heart and you're connected to the people around you. But what about *you*? Don't you deserve that same level of care and connection with yourself? Pouring that love into others can't last when you aren't consistently pouring it back into you first.

ADD BOUNDARIES TO SUBTRACT STRESS

Often we say yes when our energy is telling us to say no. We say "sure" when we aren't sure. But why? Not all of us are trapped by worry and guilt. But some of us feel it's what we need to do in order to "keep the peace." But let me ask you something: Are you really keeping the peace when you throw your own peace out the window? Does it make sense to help others keep *their* peace when doing that is the direct cause of you eliminating *yours*? You're not

I AM GOING TO CHALLENGE YOU. STRAIGHT UP. IF THIS WAS EASY, WE WOULDN'T BE HAVING THIS CONVERSATION.

keeping the peace. You're losing *your* peace, and when you lose your peace, you start a war within yourself. Nipsey Hussle said it best: "Would you rather be at peace with the world and at war with yourself? Or be at war with the world and at peace with yourself?"

Every time you don't stand on your principles, you start a war within yourself. Every time you tolerate disrespect and don't put an end to it with your boundaries, you start a war within yourself. And it doesn't stop there. Before long, that war spreads to other people. You start to resent and avoid them while pretending like you're there for them. You might even still be saying yes to them while that resentment grows and grows. Next thing you know, you're exhausted and your relationships look like war zones as you're trying to figure out what the hell happened.

As a reminder, the mission of this chapter is to help you subtract stress by adding boundaries. By giving you the power to say no, and to say it loud! When you say no to something you don't want to do—something you know doesn't work for your energy—you're actually saying yes to yourself. And you deserve that yes more than anyone else. A guilt-and-worry-free yes, I might add. It's that simple when we choose to look at it that way.

Hold up, you might be thinking. *I'm a parent, a husband, a daughter, a brother (whatever the case might be), and in some of my relationships I don't know where to set these boundaries. I can't just shut it all down and start turning my back on everyone. If I just create walls and lock them out, I'm going to lose loved ones from my life.*

You're not alone with that concern. That type of worry is what makes us reluctant to even think about boundaries in the first place. When we hear the word *boundary*, we think of national borders, chain-link fences and barbed

wire, armed guards and passport checkpoints. And sometimes your boundaries will have to be like that. But if you
do a thoughtful job of creating and communicating your
boundaries in a healthy fashion, they can work as bridges
instead of walls.

LET THE REAL ONES IN

If you have people-pleasing tendencies, you've been
giving people unrestricted access to your time and energy.
You're not protecting yourself, so it's no wonder you're
feeling drained and depleted. Now think about an old cas-
tle for a minute. It has walls, towers, and a deep moat. But
there's also a drawbridge to let people in—at the right time
and under the right circumstances. No more unwelcome
surprise visitors, right?

Okay, back to you now. Your boundaries should not
be for the purpose of keeping everyone out, all the time.
Instead they allow you to invite things and people in
under the circumstances of your own choosing. If you
need clarity in a relationship, then you invite that in; you
build a bridge so it can get to you. You say, "Here's what I
need for clarity, and here's where you can meet me with
that." Those who respect your needs and want to support
you will cross the bridge and meet you there. Those who
don't? Maybe they turn around. Maybe they fall into the
moat. Either way, they know how to cross that bridge if
and when they are ready.

So how do we go about building these boundaries and
bridges? The first step is to understand your own prior-
ities, principles, and values. What matters most to you?
What makes you feel the best? What standards do you live

by? Once you figure those out, it becomes easier to recognize when your principles and values are threatened, which makes it easier to know when to say no. In fact, many times, I tell people that it isn't really me saying no to them—it's my standards and principles.

Some of my core values are grounded in and expressed in my relationships with God, with myself, and with my family. I've decided that my mornings are for me to focus on these relationships and nothing else. So if it's not an emergency, don't call me before noon and expect me to pick up. Don't knock on my door; don't send me e-mails, texts, or DMs, unless you're okay with not hearing back from me until later that day. I start engaging with the outside world at 12 P.M. sharp, Central Time—before that, it's only the special people in my life who have access to me.

I've heard some complaints about this over the years. I often hear, "Man, Trent, it's so hard to reach you in the mornings! I had something I wanted to tell you." And I have to let them know, "Yeah, that's my time." I'll say it with warmth and a smile, but not with an apology. I don't need to apologize for anything, because the bridge to connecting with me is there for them. If they're still frustrated about it—and many have been—that's their problem. Not mine. The real ones understand.

I don't feel guilty about this, because I'm clear on why I created that boundary in the first place and why I protect it. I know that in order for me to be the best Trent for myself, my family, and my community, disconnecting from distractions during the first part of my day is something I need to stand firm on. (More on disconnecting in the next chapter.) I disconnect from the world so I can reconnect with my soul—and reconnect with my peace. Is that thing you wanted to tell me at 10 A.M. more

WHEN YOU SAY NO TO SOMETHING YOU DON'T WANT TO DO, YOU'RE ACTUALLY SAYING YES TO YOURSELF. AND YOU DESERVE THAT YES.

important than the peace in my soul? It might be to you, but it isn't to me. So sit tight, and I'll holla at you sometime in the afternoon.

INTERNAL VS. EXTERNAL BOUNDARIES

Over the years I've been able to develop strategies to protect my energy, but it wasn't always this way for me, believe me. Prior to 2009, things were pretty different. That was the year I found my true purpose. When I reflect on it now, I can see it was a damn good year, but it sure didn't start out that way—it started out with me hitting one low after another.

I had just finished the 2008 NFL season with the pro team in Washington, D.C., now known as the Commanders, when word came down that I'd been cut. It was my third cut in three years—previously, I'd been on the practice squads of the Seattle Seahawks (2007 season) and the Indianapolis Colts (2006 season). Before I'd even joined Washington, I had a strong feeling that pro football wouldn't be it for me. But it was all I'd been working on since I was five, playing Pop Warner ball in New Orleans, so when the team invited me to join their active roster, I decided I'd give it one more shot. It was all I really knew how to do at the time, or so I thought.

That last cut was the end of my dream and it left a huge hole in me. Everything I'd been working for, ever since my early days playing Pop Warner in the Louisiana humidity, was gone, just like that. *Poof.* I went from thinking I was going to able to buy mansions for me and my family to living in a room in my parents' house. I felt broken in a way that I could not even accept at first, and I had no idea how to cope with the disappointment and the uncertainty that followed.

Instead, I numbed it. I surrounded myself with friends—going out, drinking, smoking, doing plenty of things that I knew weren't good for me, sometimes five or six nights a week. Thousands of dollars racked up on my credit card every month, just partying. I wanted to continue to be a part of and provide that good time for everyone around me, even if I couldn't afford it financially or spiritually. I told myself this was "self-care." Doing what I wanted to do, going out, having fun, feeling good. (Or what I thought of at the time as "feeling good.")

This went on for months. But then one night we were out in downtown Dallas, and there was a moment when I was sitting by myself. Maybe my boys had gone to the bar for another round or they were on the dance floor or somewhere—I don't remember exactly. What I do remember was sitting there alone, wasted, and looking around at everybody else. There were people ten, fifteen years older than I was, stumbling around, faded, all there to escape whatever their daytime realities were. There was one guy in particular who looked like he was about 50. This guy was the man of the hour—everybody knew him, everybody wanted to kick it with him. Even the DJ was calling out to him between tracks. As I watched him work the room, a sudden realization hit me: I didn't want this to be my life. I didn't want to end up being him.

Let me be clear: no disrespect toward this man. I just knew that for me, this wasn't it. This was not the road to my best self. I also knew that if I didn't change, I would get addicted to the lifestyle. Addicted to the popularity, adulation, and false sense of success. And then, where would I be in another ten or twenty years? Nowhere good. For me, this scene was a college fantasy, not a life direction.

Thoughts of my son, Tristan, popped into my head. He was one and a half years old at the time, and this was no way for me to build something I could be proud to leave him with. I didn't know where to go next, but I knew my time, energy, and money were worth far more than this, and I knew I was in charge of my own destiny. I had to change.

My first real task was to do some deep interior work. I had to set some real boundaries for myself—and within myself. I had to take that dreadful first look in the mirror the next morning and say, "Trent, look man, this ain't it." I decided I was done with the nightly trips to the clubs. I'd had enough. Instead of avoiding the discomfort, the pain, that way, I'd find a way to walk right through it. That was the internal boundary I set, my promise to myself. It wasn't easy, but I was determined.

Next it was time for me to put that skill to some use, and do something even harder—make that boundary external. I had to set that same boundary with my inner circle, my ride-or-dies. My homies who had always been there for me. I had to tell them, "Look, that life isn't for me anymore."

Remember when I talked about how boundaries can be bridges just as much as they can be walls? These guys were part of my chosen family. So, instead of just pushing them out of my life, I invited them to cross a bridge with me. I told them straight up: "I want you guys in my life. Just because going out to clubs doesn't serve me anymore, that doesn't mean I don't want you around. Come work out with me and let's work on building our best life together." Some of them took me up on my offer. Others didn't—at least, not right away. I had to accept that.

That's how RehabTime was born. Filming two-minute videos in that red-walled room in my parents' house, then starting to share them and post them online. At first doing it so that I could heal, only to find out that it was starting to help others, one person at a time. Instead of the club, I started spending my late nights at the gym. I started reading, looking for insight from people who'd been through similar things, people who could teach me a way forward.

Today, I thank God for that time, because all along, He had a plan. That first moment of awareness grew into greater understanding, and I started to see that self-care is actually about making choices that lead you to become the greatest version of yourself. It's about choosing situations that are beneficial to your energy and that are beneficial to your peace. Life became a lot easier for me when I got this. It helped me define and understand my own principles. This helped me understand my real needs, which I now hold in the highest esteem. This in turn took a lot of pressure off me, because it led me to that all-important ability to set boundaries that don't budge.

SET THE TONE FOR YOUR LIFE

One of the greatest moments of my life was when I finally realized how my lack of boundaries was costing me my peace. I saw that my peace was priceless—just like yours is. But it can be hard to stand on your boundaries if you don't know how to go about creating them in the first place. It all begins with that fundamental ability to say no. N-O. Period! This is how you start to set the tone for your life.

I've heard it said that "No" is a full sentence. No further explanation needed. I like that a lot. One of the reasons we say yes to what we should be saying no to is because we think that the reasons behind our no aren't going to be good enough for the other person. We don't feel like we have an adequate answer if they push back and ask, "Why not?" Can we take a second to highlight how backward that is? That no isn't for them—it's for *you*. You're the only one who needs to be convinced of the reasoning, and if you're feeling a no, that's all the reason you need. Friendly reminder to set that internal boundary with those first cousins known as worry and guilt. As I said before, I believe worrying is a major source (a branch, if you will) of people-pleasing. Taking it a step further, that worry may be coming from insecurity (part of the root).

Nonetheless, this happens all the time. Someone asks you for your energy and then your insecurity makes you worry about keeping them comfortable. You put their needs ahead of yours, agree to their ask, then *bam!* You've just signed yourself up for something else you didn't want to be a part of. Now they've got your energy and you've just shortchanged yourself—classic people-pleasing move. But listen: You weren't created to be *misused by other people*. God created you with gifts that are meant to be *used by you*.

Once you recognize the value of *your* energy, *your* peace, you'll be able to start creating those internal boundaries—the habits and decisions that will keep you moving toward your best self. Saying no to things that drain you, and saying yes to things that support you, will make that insecurity, worry, and guilt smaller and smaller. Eventually, you'll be standing firm, feet planted, rooted in feeling more secure than ever in who you are. You'll be setting the tone!

When you stay committed and consistent with your own boundaries, you are also instructing others on how to treat you. If you've already learned to be a people-pleaser, this might seem difficult, but let me tell you something crazy about this process. Once you feel the power of saying no, setting boundaries, and sticking to them, you will quickly earn more respect from others. They may be upset at first that they no longer have unlimited access to you and can't control you anymore (even if they were doing it unintentionally). Eventually, though, most people will have more respect for you than they ever did before. Why is this? It's because we subconsciously admire people who stand up for themselves. We admire bravery, even if we don't agree with the specific stance. We all aspire to live lives of courage, so when we see courage in action, we're drawn to it, because we want to learn from people who are living courageously.

What about the ones who aren't showing you that respect? They're showing you where the toxicity is in your life. Pay attention to who respects your new boundaries, and who quietly ignores them. That's a sneaky kind of toxicity, and it might challenge your new boundary-setting skills—but that's exactly why it's so important to do this work in the first place. That's the power of your no. Get that mess out of here. The real ones will adjust and show you respect. More importantly, you'll respect yourself more.

Furthermore, saying no will create the space for you to receive the yesses that were meant for your life. (I'm gonna go ahead with the fact that *yesses* is a word, if we are good with that.) This is a key component to what I like to call a championship mindset. You have to become legendary at saying no to whatever is not bringing you your yes!

EVOLVING > EXISTING

If most of this is new to you and you're still questioning how to get started with setting boundaries, let me give you a recap. The first step is to identify the things that bring you energy and the things that drain your energy. When your energy is threatened, test out the power of your all-important no when your soul urges you to from within. Then it's time to welcome in the abundance of saying yes to yourself, to what you are actually meant to receive.

But don't expect this to be an overnight process. Start out small, and keep working at it. We are meant to evolve as humans, not merely exist. Evolving is growing. Existing is dying. Kevin Hart said in his book *The Decision*, "Everything in nature is in a state of growth or decay." As human beings, we are also always in one of these two states: growth or decay. What state are you in right now?

Whether you're just learning how to create new boundaries or you're deeper into the process of setting and communicating them, you're growing. On the other hand, if you are still allowing anything and everything to control you, I see that as a stage of decay. A slow death. Death to your energy, your mind, your soul, and your life. Death to your peace.

It wasn't easy when I first made these changes in my own life. I remember people telling me, "Man, Trent. You changed, bro. You act different." I'm not gonna lie, that hurt at first. My first instinct was to argue, defend myself, and point out that I was the same Trent I'd always been. But then I thought, *You know what? You're damn right I've changed. I'm taking care of my life, choosing myself over others, and learning my worth. I'm done with accepting less than I should, and I'm done being used.*

WE ARE ALWAYS IN ONE OF TWO STATES: GROWTH OR DECAY. WHICH STATE ARE YOU IN RIGHT NOW?

Yeah, I've changed, and I'm going to keep changing, too. I choose growth over decay. And I highly recommend you do the same.

FAMILY FIRST?

Anyone else ever deal with Mom, Dad, siblings, or relatives asking for this or that? Popping up in the house anytime they want to? Overextending their welcome by a massive long shot? Friends and loved ones can often do these things, too. If life was a video game, these people might be known as the Peace Invaders! (Ha ha.)

You might be wondering why I put a question mark in the title of this section. Let me explain. I'm all about "family first," but it comes with a few caveats. My family—blood and chosen—comes before almost everything else in life. But in order to keep my family a priority, I have to first prioritize my own needs so that I have a healthy amount in my cup of life to pour out for others.

Let's be careful here so this doesn't get twisted. Remember how my idea of self-care used to be hitting the club five or six nights a week? That's not what I mean when I talk about prioritizing my own needs. First, things were way out of balance for me at that time. Second, partying wasn't a true "need"—not the type of need I had to meet in order to get to my best self. I'm talking about the sorts of needs that help you grow and maintain your own energy and your resources, which are what you need to be there for the people who truly need you. You can't take care of anyone else's needs if you fail to honor yours first.

Setting boundaries with family can be especially challenging, but there are ways to do it so that you honor yourself *and* those around you. Family relationships, even difficult ones, consist of more love, more responsibility, more long-term consequences than your other relationships, so it's not quite so easy to shut family members out of your life, like you might do with others. This is where treating your boundaries as bridges comes into play most of all. I like to say that boundaries shouldn't lead to isolation, but to elevation. They should improve your relationships, your peace, and your life overall.

You can't choose your bloodline, but you *can* choose your boundaries! Yes, even with family. Boundaries with family, people who will remain in your life, might mean making slight adjustments. Just as in any other relationship—personal, professional, or beyond—communication will be the rudder of your ship. *Unclear communication will always lead to unfair expectations.* Think about the messages you've shared with those you're closest to. Have you clearly communicated your boundaries with them, or are you just assuming they should be mind readers? If you aren't communicating your boundaries, how could anyone respect them? Once you figure out your core principles and values, and what you need to protect your energy and peace, find the time for respectful, calm conversations about this with the people closest to you. It might not be easy, but avoiding difficult conversations out of worry is what leads to depletion in the first place, remember? The time is now to put yourself first.

THE GIFT OF RESPONSIBILITY

Listen to me carefully on this: *It is acceptable to help people, but it's unacceptable to enable them.* Helping someone once—or a few times if they are struggling—cool. But what about doing this daily for months or years when they clearly aren't working as hard for themselves as you are for them? That's when you become an enabler. You enable them by showing them it's okay not to put in the work. That isn't help. In fact, it contributes to keeping them stuck in a situation that isn't working for them. You are making them depend more on you than on themselves and God. This is when it's time for that "no" to come into play.

Easier said than done, some of you may say. And that's true, it's easier said than done—but so is everything else in the world, including getting dressed and brushing your teeth this morning. But we do these things with intention and make these adjustments to improve our lives every day, even when it's hard. What's more difficult? Having constant drains on your time and energy. Relationships can fall apart pretty quickly under these circumstances, so it stands to reason you'd need to put in some work.

Obviously, parents hold extra responsibility for our children. But even in those relationships, the principle is the same. I'll catch a fish for my kids, but my real job is to show them how to catch their own. Why is this so important? There will come a day when I won't be there. The same goes for you and the roles you play for your family members, friends, co-workers, and community. Empowering them to catch their own fish is part of setting healthy boundaries, and one that leads them to depend on God and self, rather than you or any other human.

To illustrate my point, allow me to share an instance from my own life, where I found it necessary to draw a clear boundary with my son, Tristan. If I'm being real, it was not a step I was eager to take, yet it was one that I had to take.

It had always been my pleasure to cater to Tristan's needs—getting him ready for school, cooking his breakfast, and even styling his hair. But upon his 10th birthday,

I decided that the greatest gift I could give him was not just a physical object, but the gift of responsibility. The rules were straightforward—if he desired a sumptuous breakfast, he had to learn to cook it. If he wanted to make a fashion statement at school, he had to pick his own outfit. Of course, he stumbled out of the blocks—we had a few near-misses with house fires—but now, he whips up pancakes so fluffy they could float away, and his eggs are nothing short of a culinary masterpiece. The title of "breakfast maestro" in the Shelton household has been rightfully claimed by Tristan himself.

So, you might ask, how did establishing this boundary benefit *me*? It gave me the gift of time. By empowering Tristan to handle his own business, by teaching him how to catch his own fish, I gained the freedom to concentrate my mornings on protecting my peace. And from setting this firm yet loving boundary, I also got the satisfaction of giving invaluable support to my son.

LONG-TERM EFFECTS

When I decided to get off the Excess Express, I created boundaries for myself. I then shared them with my crew, but I included that bridge to stay connected with me and my new direction. Like I said, some of them understood and were cool with it, and came along. Some didn't, though, and I had to say good-bye to a few friends who'd meant a lot to me. I never judged them for it. They were just in different places in their lives. I'm not gonna lie, though—it was painful.

But here's the crazy part, and one of the reasons I know God is real and works in mysterious but purposeful ways for sure: Some of those friends I lost came back into contact with me a few years later and actually thanked me. They weren't on the same page as I was at first, but after traveling their own journeys, they came to appreciate the decision I'd made and were grateful that I'd set an example of how to have fun and be successful in healthier ways. That was truly an unexpected gift, especially due to the pain I felt during the time we were disconnected, and it helped me heal even more. God's work.

Bottom line: once you know what your heart of hearts is telling you to do, you have to listen, even if it means going another way from family or friends. You might have to create some distance, and love some people from afar for a time. Who knows—those same people might come back into your life later on for a greater purpose.

CHOOSE YOURSELF

Saying it one more time for the people in the back! The first skill you need for energy protection is an ability to create and stand on your boundaries. Know what you truly need to be healthy and choose to protect yourself, rather than enabling others. But remember that unless others force you to create walls, boundaries can and should be bridges. Bridges of higher elevation, for you and them. Bridges of higher expectations, for your life and for theirs.

Not everyone will accept that invitation. Not everyone will cross those bridges. That's fine. One of my personal mantras is: *I would rather be viewed as coldhearted than live brokenhearted*. If the world you were brought up in made you into something of a people-pleaser, setting boundaries won't be easy at first. That's okay, too. If you're reading this, though, it means you've had enough, and you're willing to make changes.

At the start and end of each day, we all have something in common: choices. Saying yes is a choice. Saying no is a choice. Setting boundaries is a choice. Me choosing me is a choice. You choosing you is a choice. Happiness is a choice. Peace, my friend, is also a choice. *Choose wisely.*

Protect Your Peace Practice

Focus on your core values

Now that you have read about what it takes to create and stand on your boundaries, take a second and think about what your core values are.

I mentioned in this chapter how my relationship with God, with myself, and with my family represent some of my deepest core values. Within those relationships, honesty is key for keeping the relationships healthy.

What is something you value in *your* relationships? (If you need help pinpointing what you value, remember what we talked about earlier in the chapter: identify what brings you energy and what drains it.)

Who is one person you can practice setting a boundary with to help you draw closer to what you value most (and maybe help them do the same)?

DISCONNECT OFTEN

*I think a winner has to be a master of preparation;
they have to be a master of connection, extremely
competitive, and have really high standards for
themselves and the people around them.*

— MAYA MOORE

Have you ever been on vacation, maybe at the beach, and decided to treat yourself by watching a sunset after a day full of doing what you love with the people you love? Man, I'm telling you, there's nothing quite like standing on the shoreline, watching the sun dip below the horizon, and feeling the day's warmth fade away.

And how about waking up early enough on that vacation to connect your soul to the salt in the air, the waves drifting in, and the sun rising like a perfect finish to a freshly painted canvas? I'm talking about getting up before the rest of the world and witnessing the beauty of the world as it wakes up around you. Feeling the cool morning breeze on your skin, hearing the waves crashing against the shore, and watching the sun peek over the horizon.

Starting the morning with a sunrise reminds me that I have been gifted another day. Another day to live my purpose, to spend time with my loved ones, and to make an impact in the world. It's a reminder that each day is a gift and that we should make the most of it.

Now, maybe you won't have a beach nearby every day, but catching the sunrise each morning and the sunset each evening are two of my favorite ways of connecting to what truly matters in life. Rituals like these are about taking the time to appreciate the beauty of the world around us and being mindful of our connections to it.

Starting and finishing the day by paying attention to what we are connected to—and what we should disconnect *from*—can be a game-changer. It helps us to stay focused on what's truly important and to let go of anything that may be holding us back.

CHOOSING YOUR CONNECTIONS

Our lives reflect not only our choices but also the connections we have created due to those choices. This is a powerful realization that can help us take ownership of our lives and make intentional choices that align with our values and goals. When I think about connections, I've found that we are often either connected to what brings us life or to what drains our life. It's like we have an energy meter, and each connection either adds to it or takes away from it. Think about your decisions and connections and how you spend your time. Are you giving your energy to things or people that bring you joy and fulfillment, or are you spending time on things that leave you feeling drained and unfulfilled?

I've seen that many people are very in tune with the things that bring them life. Doing what you love, with who you love. It's the simple things, like catching that sunrise, making time for a good workout or a favorite meal, or spending time with close friends. These things energize us and fill us with purpose and meaning.

And when you give your energy to something or someone who is meant for your life and will reciprocate your energy, your energy multiplies. That connection with someone is known as *synergy*—combining powers, Captain Planet style. Think of these people as generators, as they help you generate, increase, and multiply your energy.

Of course, it can work the other way, too.

Every day, we face countless small moments that may not seem like a big deal, but they can mount up to become a weight that can crush us. Sure, the big things are obvious—health problems, relationship issues, you name it. But the subtle, unnoticed things can be the most dangerous and the biggest threat to our peace. They're the "thousand tiny cuts," quietly chipping away at our joy and well-being, leaving us drained and disconnected from our true selves. Whether it's scrolling through social media and starting your day out with drama, conflict, and unhealthy comparisons, or being in toxic relationships that sap your energy, the effects of these small things add up. When you give your energy to the things or people not meant for your life, it's like pouring your energy into a garbage disposal, flipping the switch, and watching your peace disintegrate right before your eyes.

You cannot afford to allow these things to dominate your life. Toxic people, habits, and environments can drag us down, little by little, until we become strangers to ourselves. I need you to feel me on this: We don't have forever. We can't waste our precious time on this earth pouring our energy into things or people that only drain us dry. If we keep on investing in negativity, we put our mental health in jeopardy. We risk falling into a cycle of stress, depression, and unhappiness that can consume us whole. Make no mistake, stress is a ruthless serial killer that will stalk you in silence until it murders your peace.

This chapter will help you become an even more vigilant protector of your energy. No more giving it away for free. No more wasting it on things or people that serve no purpose. Repeat after me: "Not anymore!" From this day forward, anyone who wants a piece of your energy better be ready to earn, respect, and cherish it. No more freebies. You deserve to be selective about whom you let into your life and what you invest your energy in. It's time to raise the bar.

A SPACE FOR GROWTH

When I first wake up in the morning, I consciously disconnect from the world's noise to connect with the most important person in my life: myself. To do that, I disconnect from social media and any other influences that may not be healthy for me at that moment. And let me tell you: it's a straight non-negotiable for me.

How many of us rely on external sources to fill us up daily? How many of us start our mornings diving into other people's lives on our phones or doing tasks for others instead of connecting with ourselves? How many of us are connected to entities that make us feel powerless, and then we wonder why we don't feel powerful? Too many.

WE CAN'T WASTE
OUR PRECIOUS
TIME ON THIS
EARTH POURING
OUR ENERGY INTO
THINGS OR PEOPLE
THAT ONLY DRAIN
US DRY.

And I'm here to tell you it's time to pull the damn plug! Excuse my French—I'm fired up about this. We need to let go of the things in our lives that don't connect us to the higher version of ourselves. We must cut the cords that keep us tethered to negativity, distraction, and outside influences.

When I started connecting to what was going on *inside* me, that's when things got real. To disconnect from everything that was draining my energy and connect with just the things I needed. It was challenging. It took practice. It took discipline. But I knew I had to do it to create a new soul momentum for my life. So I developed a habit of waiting at least an hour to check my phone in the morning (like I mentioned in the last chapter). I disconnected from social media and the rest of the world and focused on clearing my headspace. And that's when the greatness started to happen. I started asking myself, "What do I need in my life to regain my energy? What will increase my happiness? What will provide me peace?" Those questions became the foundation for my transformation.

The ultimate power lies in disconnecting from the noise and chaos of our external environment and instead focusing on getting right with ourselves. This involves being real with yourself and asking the fundamental question of "What do I need?" Once I committed to resisting distractions, I began experiencing the inner peace we all seek. I found solace in reciting affirmations that reinforced my worthiness: *"I am peace. I am love. I am happiness. I am free."* These affirmations can transform our thought patterns, rewire our subconscious mind, elevate our beliefs, and unleash a wave of positive energy. After all, if we don't speak these truths into our existence, how can we expect to experience them?

Connecting with myself was a transformative journey that opened the door to a deeper spiritual connection with God. Whether on my knees in prayer, meditating in a quiet space, or hitting the trails in nature, these practices became the foundation of my formula for creating and protecting my peace. So let me ask *you* something: What prevents you from experiencing that deep spiritual connection and inner tranquility? What external distractions must you disconnect from to return to your true self?

It's time to break away and redirect your focus toward internal growth. How can you shift your daily routine to prioritize what truly matters? How can you cultivate that deep, internal connection from your waking moments until you shut it down for the night? If you commit to this process with some solid intention, there is no doubt that you will align with the person you were created to be.

PLUG INTO PURPOSE

When I step out in the morning and witness the sun rising, I don't just see the light illuminating the sky. I see a reminder from God that He has awakened me with a divine purpose in mind. I reflect on the times when I was lost and unsure of my path, but then I aligned myself with my purpose and everything changed. As those first rays of light hit my face, I feel an overwhelming sense of gratitude because I know what it's like to struggle with finding purpose. And if you're going through the same thing, I'm here to tell you that you are not alone.

People always ask me, "Trent, how do I find my purpose?" My response: "Save yourself some Google searches—stop searching for it—and remember these three words: *I am purpose.*" You are a living, breathing manifestation of divine purpose. Against all odds, you were brought into this world on purpose and for a purpose, and that's a miracle in itself. My morning routine—phone down; sun up— helps me plug into my purpose. It pushes out the external and creates space for me to tune in to the internal, which is much harder to discern. Ram Dass said it beautifully: "The quieter you become, the more you can hear."

If you're feeling lost and separated from your purpose, it's time to do some soul-searching. Take a deep breath and ask yourself: What must you disconnect from to reconnect with what truly matters? How much of your precious time is spent doing things you love, surrounded by people you love? And if your answers leave you feeling unfulfilled, it's time to make a change. The journey toward purpose won't be easy, but it's worth it. It's worth the risk, the uncertainty, and the uncomfortable moments of growth. Because at the end of the day, the greatest gift you can give your soul is a life lived on purpose.

Let me set the record straight real quick on one thing. Many people make the mistake of confusing purpose with *placement.* I see it all the time at the Protect Your Peace Retreats that I lead: people think that getting into the right school, landing the right job, or finding the perfect relationship is the key to unlocking their purpose. But after a half-day with me, they quickly realize the idea that "purpose is placement" is a lie. A straight-up *myth.* True purpose is not about validation from the outside. Your purpose can't be found in a job title, a relationship status, or other external factors. It's already within you, waiting to be tapped into. Write this down on the tablet of your heart: *You don't find your purpose—you align with it.* And once you truly understand those words, everything else falls into place. So don't waste another minute chasing after placement. Focus on connecting with your purpose and let that be your guiding force.

PLUG INTO NATURE

Watching the sun rise and set is just the beginning of my love affair with nature. My connection to the natural world runs deep, and it's one of the cornerstones of protecting my peace. I truly believe nature heals. When I'm out there, surrounded by the breathtaking beauty of the world, I feel like a different person, and it brings out a different energy within me. The way the sun filters through the trees, the scent of fresh pine in the air, and the sound of the wind rustling through the leaves—it all works together to create a feeling of pure serenity. My allergies don't love it, but my soul can't get enough of it. It's like nature can release something from my soul and bring me back to my true self.

And when I'm out there walking or doing my trail runs, listening to the birds, feeling the air change with the elevation, and experiencing the changing seasons on the plains of Texas, I take on a new identity. In these times, I call myself "Nature Shells," because I feel like a different being. It's like I'm tapping into some primal part of myself that I didn't even know existed. I've done everything out in nature. I've hugged trees, taken naps, and even lifted rocks as my weights. There's something truly special about connecting with nature in such a raw and unfiltered way. It's like I'm tapping into some ancient wisdom forgotten in our modern world. It's a reminder of our connection to the earth and the incredible strength and resilience that comes from being in harmony with nature.

One of my all-time favorite ways to disconnect from the busyness of life and connect with my soul is by deliberately tapping into this Nature Shells mode. Here's what I do: I lace up my trail shoes, put some peaceful instrumentals with my headphones on low so I can still hear the sounds of nature, and man, it's like I'm transported to a whole other world. A place where problems can't find me. It's like my body and mind shift into a different gear. I feel calmer, more centered, and more at peace. I feel like it's the greatest prescription for one's mental health.

When I awoke to my purpose, I realized that one of my callings was sharing nature's benefits with others. At the time, I was really getting rolling with my podcast and discovering how I could use social media to share the love, but then COVID-19 hit, and it plunged me into the depths of stress. I couldn't move (physically or metaphorically) like I am used to, so I had to switch things up a bit. Instead of recording my content in an office, I made nature my office.

Let me take you on a trip inside my head for a minute. I'm imagining myself out on a trail run, with a table set up in the middle of the trail. And what's on the table, you ask? Only a "Protect Your Peace" banner, my friend! Can you picture it? Me, recording myself talking, maybe even interviewing a few birds or a local coyote. LMAO! I know, I know, it sounds crazy. But I haven't actually done it yet . . . emphasis on the *yet*.

In all seriousness, when I'm out in nature, I'm just disconnecting from all the external noise and getting in tune with what's happening inside me. And when I feel centered, I hit "live" on my phone and start sharing my wisdom with the world. And you know what? People started connecting with me left and right, telling me I've inspired them to get out in nature and find peace.

So if you're feeling stressed or overwhelmed, take a cue from my girl Mary Davis and go for a walk in nature. As she says, "A walk in nature, walks the soul back home." And who knows, maybe you'll even run into a few birds or a coyote who wants to be interviewed. Hey, it could happen!

Now, I want to touch on something else important here. You might be thinking, *Trent, you can have nature, bro—that ain't me. That's for the birds, man—literally.* And let's be real, as a Black guy, I know that many of us weren't exactly raised on the nature life. But I'm not here to force you to love nature like I do. I get it. Some of y'all might not be about that life. And that's cool; no judgment here. I'll be the first to admit it: I may love nature, but I don't love everything in nature. I have some scary stories about bobcats, bears, deer, you name it. Keepin' it straight-up as I always do with y'all—if I am on a walk or a trail run and the bushes start shaking, you best believe I'm taking off like a bat outta hell. I might even beat my NFL combine 40-yard dash time.

Still, if you're one of those people who haven't yet experienced the power of nature, then my guess is that you just haven't given it a real try. It's like when my kids say they don't like a new food before they even try it— you've gotta take a bite and see for yourself!

So I'm here to urge you to get yourself some decent shoes, download the AllTrails app, and hit up some trails in your area. Trust me, the app will keep you safe and guide you to the best routes, photos, and descriptions. And if you can find someone to join you, even better. Bonus points if they have some experience with the great outdoors.

Almost everyone I know who's given it a try has experienced some version of what I feel every time I'm out there in nature: the mental health boost, the clarity, the release of unwanted emotions. It's truly a gift from God.

I'm passionate about this because of what it brought to my life. Nature isn't cutting me a check for this advertising, but it has paid me in priceless ways. So come on, take a bite, try it, and let nature work its magic on you. Your soul will never be the same.

ENVIRONMENTS HOLD ENERGY

I've just given you an earful about the power of the natural environment. What's also important to know is that just as nature holds abundance and positivity for the soul, other environments can hold negative energy. Are you in an environment where you are always stressed out, or where you are not appreciated? Has that led to you not appreciating yourself?

My office became a stress-filled environment when COVID-19 had us social-distancing, so I had to take further action and make nature my office for a time. You might not have that same luxury. And even in the best of times, many of us have to show up to jobs that stress us out to take care of ourselves and our families. I truly get it; I've been there. I know what it's like to feel trapped in a situation that drains the life out of you. But I also know there are ways to carve out time for yourself, even with a demanding schedule. Take a step back and look for those gaps in your day. Find those moments when you can disconnect from the stress and connect with yourself. Even when you can't change your situation, you can change *who you are in the situation*. My wise grandmothers used to say, "You can choose who you are in any situation. So never give power to the things trying to make you feel powerless." Granny Bone and Mother Shelton were women of great wisdom, and their words have stayed with me my whole life. And let me tell you, they were a thousand percent right. *Don't ever let external factors become the determining factor in how you feel about yourself.* You hold the power to rise above any situation and continue to do what's right for you. Stay true to yourself, my friend, and don't let the world's noise drown out your voice. Keep moving forward with conviction, and you'll naturally outgrow anything that tries to hold you back.

Once you get used to shifting your mindset in this direction, you will gain a whole new peace within yourself. And man, that peace is priceless. I'm talking about new paths of life, new ways of thinking, new ways of moving, and new levels of greatness. Quiet the outside noise to start tapping into what is uniquely yours. Disconnect often. Disconnect from distractions. Disconnect from negative environments. Disconnect from anything that's taking away from your *peace.*

THE RUNNING CLOCK

Have you ever held the belief that our days will just continue? It's easy to believe that tomorrow will always be there. After all, we've been waking up each day for as long as we can remember. But the truth is, tomorrow is never promised. Forever comes with an expiration date.

It's a realization that hits us like a ton of bricks when we lose someone close to us. I know this all too well because it has happened to me many times.

Time stops for no one. We are all on a running clock that's impossible to pause or rewind. And no matter how successful or powerful we may be, Father Time is undefeated. Even guys like Tom Brady, Lebron James, and Tony Robbins are not immune to the ticking clock.

If you've been running around like you've got all the time in the world, it probably means you're putting off your connections to your purpose while staying connected to things dragging you down. It's time to stop all that and connect to the actual reality we all live in.

It's easy to get used to the many distractions the modern world presents. Pick up that phone first thing in the morning and scroll through social media for an hour—tick-tock. Flip through the channels, hoping you find something good to watch—tick-tock. Hang out with people who don't serve your purpose—tick-tock. But who wants to get to the end of life and look back on hours of purposeless distractions and wasted energy? I know I don't.

Y'all know I'm an athlete. Football is four 15-minute quarters, and that's it. If you're trailing at the end of 60 minutes, game over. You take the L and head back into that sad, depressed, quiet locker room. I'm a basketball head, too—I played on various teams as a kid, mostly during football off-seasons. NBA, same thing: four 12-minute quarters, and then that buzzer goes off. What's done is done. You can't go back and take that open three-pointer you passed up. You can't go back for that extra burst of speed on defense that would have let you close down someone's lane.

You get the point. This is a way to think about our reality in life. Everyone is on a running clock, so you need to disconnect from thinking you'll have time to write that poem for your significant other . . . tomorrow. Disconnect from thinking you'll have time to chase your dreams later down the road. Disconnect from waiting to call your mom to tell her you love her because you think you can catch up later in the week. When these impulses come to you, act on them! Doing so—*today*—will connect you to the

STAY TRUE TO YOURSELF, MY FRIEND, AND DON'T LET THE WORLD'S NOISE DROWN OUT YOUR VOICE.

things that add to your life. Neglecting them will snatch portions of your life away from you. Remember: *Everything is temporary.* I'm not trying to put fear in your heart—I'm trying to put reality and purpose in your mind.

MAKING DEATH A REALITY

I want to make sure you know that I don't take death lightly. In fact, as I was writing these words, I was in one of the deepest periods of grief I have ever experienced, which started after my mother and grandmother passed away in 2021. So don't ever think that I am making light of our mortality. If you're struggling with something similar, I feel you.

When we lose someone close, we may be tempted to stop living ourselves because the pain is so great. But we can also choose to move forward and live in a way that will honor our loved one's life. I love the TED Talk from writer and podcaster Nora McInerny—even her title alone is profound: "We don't 'move on' from grief. We move forward with it."

That sums it all up. Moving forward without denying or ignoring. If our loved ones in Heaven could have one more wish for us, it would be to see us moving forward graciously with intention after taking the necessary time to heal. Turning that pain into strength. Turning our worst nightmare into the achievement of our greatest dreams. Letting that loss impart a greater sense of urgency and using that sense of urgency to empower us to disconnect from whatever is wasting our time. When we clear that space, we can dedicate it to doing what matters with those who matter.

The alternative is one of the scariest words in the English language: *regret.* One of my favorite motivational speakers, Les Brown, offers a powerful visualization to illustrate this. I'll share it here, but I highly recommend you look into it and hear it from the man himself. Les suggests that you visualize yourself on your deathbed. First, check in with what questions you might have on your mind. Did you know what you wanted to achieve? Did you succeed?

Now imagine yourself surrounded by different versions of yourself in the form of ghosts. Everything you could have been or might have been, everything you ever dreamed about. Doctors, lawyers, speakers, teachers, professional athletes—you fill in the blank. Now listen to what these ghosts have to say to you. They might say, "We gave you these ideas for a reason. We came to you hoping you would make these gifts come to life. Why didn't you ever go for it? Why did you wait until death to regret not making your dreams come true?"

What gifts are you ignoring and keeping locked up inside you? What gifts are buried because of procrastination, pain, lack of forgiveness, distraction, et cetera? There is a reason that little voice inside you sometimes screams to come out in the form of your greatness. There is a reason you daydream or have dreams at night about the *greatest you* and what that can truly look like in this lifetime.

I will put this as simply as possible: Go after it while you can, before it's too late. Why live for what anyone else wants? Even if it's not what your boss or loved ones want for you. This is your life. Connect to *you*, not *them.* You weren't created with gifts just for you to leave them wrapped up. Those gifts were placed in your heart so you can share them with the world. Not tomorrow. Today. The world needs them.

ENERGY IS EXPENSIVE

Listen, my friend, I need you to be more than just present right now. I need you to be *super* locked in because I'm about to take you on a deeper dive through one of the most important points in this chapter. I need you to feel me on this before we move on. So far, I've talked about wasting time on external factors, like negative environments and relationships. But it isn't just about the time you're wasting. The real problem is the energy you waste on those unproductive connections—and *energy is expensive*!

Let's talk briefly about the evolution of "Morning Trent," the difference between who I used to be vs. who I am now. Picture the old Trent waking up with groggy eyes, reaching straight for the phone, and getting lost in the hypnotic dance of scrolling through social media. For a whole hour, submerged in online chaos, drowning in comparison and inviting unwanted negativity into my soul. The new Morning Trent wakes up, thanks God, makes a glass of hot lime Celtic salt water, and heads to the back patio for an hour to embrace his new beginning with the sunrise. I can't lie; after spending that hour of my morning scrolling, I felt drained. I struggled to shake off the weight of discontent. Comparison depleted my spirit. And even when I finally put the phone down, it was hard to shake off that heaviness and be productive. My energy was lower than a phone battery at 1 percent, clinging to its last breath of life before shutting down completely. But I found my charger in the form of starting my day off with that hour of fresh air, sunlight, and gratitude. I call this my *Peace Combo*. It replenishes my soul, overflows my cup, and powers me up to conquer my day. This is why I say that your choices *multiply your energy*. Multiply what

IF IT ISN'T A "HELL YEAH" FOR ME, THEN IT'S A "HELL NO."

you've got by a negative, and deplete yourself. Multiply it by a positive, and you're on your way to being your best self every time.

It's time to stop wasting your energy on people, environments, and things that aren't deserving and that don't multiply your positivity. Just like I talked about in Chapter 1, on boundaries, I don't care if people start calling you stuck up, or say you've changed or that you're different. Because you are changing. You are different. You are making your energy, and ultimately your peace, a top priority. If they find that threatening, then they aren't there to help you align with your greatest self, and it's time to stop making that investment.

I want you to visualize your energy like water in a bottle. You only get a finite amount of it each day. Every time you decide to pour some of that water out on something or someone that didn't deserve it, didn't appreciate it, or reciprocate it—it's gone. You lose. Period. You've thrown away a little piece of your priceless life and don't get it back. Getting back to the basketball metaphors—that's a flagrant foul. Against yourself!

It's bad enough to do it once or twice, but many of us make a habit of it. We do it daily. But the good news is that we are shedding light on this. We are creating awareness, and awareness is the first step toward transformation.

GREAT OPPORTUNITIES

Hopefully, it's getting more obvious to you what's draining your energy and how it is a must to start making those changes. I've been loud and clear, telling you to start disconnecting from the things that don't serve you. But hold up: I'm about to take it a step further. Brace yourself, 'cause this one's gonna raise some eyebrows for sure. *I also want you to say no to things that are good for you.*

You might be thinking, *What the hell are you talking about now, Trent?* Don't trip; lemme explain.

The life that God has bestowed on me comes with many opportunities. While I have deep gratitude for them all, more often than not, I have to say no to them. The rule is simple: If it isn't a "hell yeah" for me, then it's a "hell no." (Now I'm not rude like that and would never say that to anyone out loud, but you get what I'm sayin'.) If my response to an opportunity is, "That sounds like it might be okay," that isn't good enough. If my response is, "Well, I don't have anything better going on that day," that isn't good enough either. If the opportunity does not truly move me, I'm not moving with it. If I only want greatness, I can't celebrate average. Embracing mediocrity is not the life I want to live.

It should be the same for you. If an opportunity doesn't speak to your soul, why mess with it? If you don't feel that "hell yeah" energy in the opportunity, it should probably be a "hell no," and let it pass. Just keepin' it straight-up.

Some of us have been saying yes too much to things that seem okay or average. And I get it, believe me. There's safety and comfort in playing it small in life and taking the safe route. Striving for greatness can be scary. It comes with some stress and anxiety. But you didn't pick up this book to hear about being average, because you know you were made for more. Nelson Mandela said it best: "There is no passion to be found playing small—in settling for a life that is less than the one you are capable of living."

I want you to experience the shift in disconnecting from this: in letting go of good, letting go of average, and breaking free from settling for less. If you're overthinking all the stress that can come when you're pursuing greatness, fair enough. But guess what, my friend? I can guarantee you that embracing average and avoiding your greatness will lead to more regret than you can handle, and I can't think of anything more stressful than that.

So prepare yourself for greatness. Understand that when you say yes to good, you say no to great. When you say yes to average, you say no to legendary. Just sayin'.

YOUR LIFE IS SOIL

I've got a friend named Ed Mylett, a colleague and a fellow traveler in this space of wellness, speaking, and podcasting. (If you aren't familiar with him, please check out his stuff—I love his work.) During one of our interviews, Ed asked me what to do when we have toxic people or things in our lives. What do we do about these energy drainers, these robbers of peace? I responded with an analogy.

Imagine your life as soil. Your surroundings, the people in it, and everything you go through—that's your soil. Your energy is like a powerful seed. If you plant it in toxic soil, it won't flourish. It won't bear fruit. Now picture planting that seed in healthy soil. Soil that's going to nurture and help you harvest the blessings you deserve. It's as simple as that. The right choice here paves the way to a life filled with peace and joy. If you aren't feeling those things, check your soil. Where are you planting your seed? Disconnect from the things that drain your energy and deplete your peace. Connect to wholesome environments that nourish and inspire you to thrive. Remember this: *Bad soil creates death. Good soil creates life.*

Protect Your Peace Practice

What will you disconnect from?

It should seem clear now how important it is to disconnect, often. What you choose to disconnect from will be your choice, my friend.

I want you to be creative, but one easy example (hint) would be disconnecting from your phone for a period of time when you first wake up, as well as before bed at night. No phone for the first hour in the morning and for one hour before falling asleep?

When we take something away, it is often just as important to think about what we replace it with. In the case of the phone, maybe you spend time meditating and/or praying in the first and last hour of your day.

You could also spend it taking in the sunrise or sunset in nature, as we've discussed how important environments are to our peace. Maybe, just maybe, you spend the time in nature while meditating and/or praying.

I am giving you some ideas, but again, I want you to have the freedom to let these ideas guide you, or allow your inner voice that may have spoken to you during the chapter to guide you in your own unique direction on how disconnecting will work for you.

I would love for you to tag me in your socials regarding how you did on this! @TrentShelton

DEMAND YOUR WORTH

When you know yourself, you are empowered.
When you accept yourself, you are invincible.

— TINA LIFFORD

We have countless ways of calculating our status: wealth, relationships, job titles, social media followers, the homes we live in and the cars we drive, and a thousand other things. But all of these things rely on the opinions of others—they've got nothing to do with your actual worth, which was given to you at birth. It's really that simple: You are one of one.

I need you to understand something: *Who you are has nothing to do with what you have or don't have.* You see, you are a miracle. The odds that you would be born are so astronomical that the mere fact you are here and able to read this book is like winning the lottery every day for your whole life. When you realize how rare you are, you will start to see that your worth is just as rare—and it's something nobody can take away. You were created with the intention that you would be a light, and it's time to let it shine! My favorite Bible verse is Jeremiah 29:11, because it's such a strong reminder of just this. "'For I know the plans I have for you,' declares the Lord, 'plans to prosper you and not to harm you, plans to give you hope and a future.'" For me, this prosperity, this God-granted future, starts with *worth*.

I know we talk about this all the time. You've heard it before: Know your worth, then add tax. All that. Which is great. But how do we really discover our worth? Where does it live? What is your self-esteem connected to? Social media? The news? Your parents? Your significant other or possibly an ex? Your friends? Your job or your boss? Your past? Does it really come from inside you, or is someone else pulling the strings in your life and acting as your puppet master?

Take it from me—you don't have to *be* anything different than what you already are in order to *make* a difference. You are worthy already. You don't need someone else's platform when you realize *you are the platform*. I was rejected by platform after platform until I stood on my own. Knowing who you are will allow you to stand firm in your worth and live in peace, even when external circumstances are unfavorable. This is a critical component in the *Protect Your Peace* prescription, and a necessary skill to protect your energy. In fact, knowing your worth is the single biggest difference between *where you are* and *where you deserve to be*. If you find there's a difference between those two things for you, then lean in.

THE FOUNDATION

The first step toward a solid understanding of your worth is to build a strong foundation for it, and that starts with *acceptance*. When I hit rock bottom and spent years digging into my root issues, I discovered that this was the main thing preventing me from moving forward. I didn't accept myself. Take note: the key word there is *I*. It didn't matter what other people thought of me, and it doesn't matter what other people think of you—acceptance means *you* are good with you. Exactly who you are, right now. In all aspects, positive and negative. Not just when you're at your best, but also when you're at your worst. Now here's the key point: Once you're able to accept yourself, you can also accept your past; and once you can accept your past, you can let it go and create a new future for yourself. At that point, you're no longer a prisoner of the past. No longer in the prison of outside opinions. No longer in the prison of failure. When you have fully accepted yourself, you take the power away from others in order to control your own narrative. That's the magical pivot, right there—from a past that was controlled by others to a future controlled by *you*. At that point, you're no longer controlled by perceived limitations. Instead, your life will be guided by your aspirations.

That's what happened for me. Once I accepted where I was coming from, I could accept where I was, and that gave me clarity on my direction. That took me to the second step of my self-worth foundation: *confidence*. The more I accepted my own abilities and qualities, the more self-assurance I found in myself. The same will occur for you. *True confidence is a reflection of knowing your worth.* It isn't about being liked, it's being content whether you are liked or not. Reach that point, and your foundation will be earthquake-proof.

STATUS VS. WORTH

To be clear, I'm talking about *you* knowing your worth. I've said it before, but it's worth repeating. When other people see how great you are, that's status. Sure, that can feel good, but it's all external. Status may put a Band-Aid over your insecurities, but it won't fill the void that is created when you forget that you were given your worth at birth. The status the world gives you can be taken away in the blink of an eye. The real goal is for you to know your own worth and step into how great you already are. Real worth can't be taken away.

I coach youth football now, and I talk to my players about this all the time. Sometimes I hear them call themselves losers after taking a single loss. I have to remind them that one game is a moment, and their worth isn't tied to winning or losing that one game. That one loss affects their team's status in a temporary football league; it's not a measure of who they are as individuals. It's the same for you. Your circumstances shouldn't be the foundation of your self-esteem, whether we're talking about a loss in a football game or something else that didn't break your way. These are all external factors. Every team, no matter how hard they train, will eventually come up against a team that's bigger, faster, or more skilled.

Maybe you've had your own share of things not going your way—a job opening that went to someone else, a romantic partner who left you for someone else. All external factors. Now I'm not saying they shouldn't hurt. When my NFL dreams came tumbling down, I went through hell. But once I found my acceptance, my confidence came back, and then I connected with my worth in a way nobody could touch. So why live this life ignoring

YOU TELL PEOPLE HOW TO TREAT YOU BY WHAT YOU ACCEPT.

what truly matters, by chasing what doesn't serve you? The world can't give you what God already gave you. Your internal peace and your inherent worth are more valuable than anything the external world has to say about you.

I do want to be clear on this, though. I'm not telling you to settle and stop striving. Go for it all. There's nothing wrong with achieving more and taking your life to higher heights. Just be clear on *what* you're striving for and *why* you're striving for it. If it's status you're after, you're never going to have enough of it. If it's the greater manifestation of your own true being, though, then that's a whole different thing. That's the future and the purpose God is talking about in the verse from Jeremiah that I quoted earlier. You're worth it, not because of what you achieve, but because of who you are.

PURSUE PEACE—NOT PERFECTION

So many people are chasing perfection, which may mean putting off living their true purpose because they feel like the timing or the circumstances aren't perfect just yet. I believe people pick up this tendency from the fake "perfection" we see on social media daily. Highlight reels of all smiles instead of the real feelings in the background. I know social media can be used in a positive way, and it has helped my professional life so much, but it can and does mess with our minds. Research has shown that social media is a factor in rising levels of depression.[2, 3, 4] It only takes a second to pop open an app, see a video of someone who's killing it out there, and end up feeling crappy about where you are in life.

Have you counted yourself out because you have had imperfect moments? Do you let your mistakes hold you back? You need to forget all that. Perfection isn't even real, and pretending like you're perfect will actually alienate people. It's not relatable! Those who strive for it and pretend they've attained it might seem impressive in a 20-second post on social media, but that's a false goal. It's easy to lose yourself in the pursuit of it, and the inevitable failure can cause massive damage to your sense of worth.

So forget the comparisons. We were born to be real, not perfect. Tapping into who you truly are and sharing that with the world is how you can create a real impact. Think about it. Who watches a movie about someone living a perfect life? That would be so boring! We live to see the setbacks that lead to comebacks, so turn your flaws into strengths by realizing that perfection is impossible—mistakes, failures, and flaws are part of the game. It's a part of the journey. You are worthy despite it all! Besides, when you own everything about yourself, it's impossible for anyone to use any of it against you. And remember, the people who might judge you aren't perfect either. No matter what kind of front they put up, they've got their own flaws and issues. So never let imperfect people make you feel like you're somehow "less" for not living up to a perfection they can't achieve themselves.

What do you do instead, then? Acknowledge, share, and *heal* from your mistakes. I've had to do this myself, and the strategies I've used include things you've already heard me talked about: therapy, journaling, exercise, spending time in nature. Through those efforts to figure things out for myself, I've found myself in a position where I have the honor and privilege of helping others. When I was growing up, my grandma would often tell me that she believed we are all "assigned" to certain people. What she meant was that you'll go through things that feel almost un-survivable at the time—and unique to you. But then later in life you'll cross paths with someone who is going through the very same thing that you have now healed from. Your new wisdom doesn't change what *you* went through, but it can sure help someone else. *Love you, Grandma, and thank you.*

To me, this is where true peace lies: walking through your pain, putting in the work and faith to heal, and then sharing your journey with others. Unfortunately, many people run away from their healing because they think that healing will be hard. Know what's harder? Living in the pain. So you can choose your "hard." One is temporary, the other lasts forever. People who choose not to start down that healing path often get so comfortable with pain that they forget that happiness is still an option. Can you identify? If you can't, it's okay. No matter what kind of accommodations you've made to keep from putting in the healing work, it's not too late to make a different choice. It's not too late to choose to flourish.

When you choose the path of healing, everything you have been through can build you. That loss you experienced? Use it for impact. The mistakes you made? Use them for learning. That huge setback? Turn it into an even bigger comeback. Remember, you make an impact every day. Whether your gifts include winning the Nobel Peace Prize or simply smiling at strangers, it's time to own them and intentionally use them for the greater good. I will go so far as to say that you owe them to the world. When you realize perfection is an illusion and accept your own worth, you can then tap into the true potential of the gift you truly are. Energy protected. Peace achieved.

HOW DO YOU DEFINE SUCCESS?

For me, the main ingredients to real success are peace and fulfillment. The moments you are at peace—or simply seeking peace—are the most fulfilling. Peace is at the top of the value charts, folks. Make it your top priority, and your best self—the greatest you—will emerge.

But as I touched on in the last section, one of the biggest blockers to peace is our tendency to compare. We look around at others' lives and find ourselves thinking, *I wish I had that job, that house, that car, that relationship,* and on and on. Here's the thing, though: You weren't meant to be a duplicate, you were meant to be an original. Why do you think we fail most when we try to act out other people's dreams?

One of the reasons I am where I am in life is because I have never been and will never be a duplicate. I'm me and forever will be. I give my voice to the world in my own unique way. I am creating my own success rather than pursuing someone else's version of success. And believe me, it hasn't always been easy. Back in 2009, when I started working in the self-development space, it was unusual and even unpopular to look like me and speak like me. Many people tried to change me on my way up. But I kept doing my thing because it was coming from my heart. I knew my worth. I knew my purpose. Eliminating comparison connected me to clarity.

Haven't you heard before that in order to make a difference, you have to *be* different, move different, act different? Maybe that thing that no one understands, that thing God placed in *your* heart, is exactly what you are supposed to be doing and sharing. You weren't called to be like everyone else, and nobody else has to approve your calling, my friend. Think about the real greats, the courageous and the brilliant, who have created real change. If they had waited on everyone's approval, they never would have accomplished anything. Copernicus went against what everyone else was saying and changed our understanding of the whole universe. Rosa Parks defied expectations and inspired the civil rights movement. Where would we be without original thinkers like them? There is a reason geniuses get the label of being crazy or being different. Sometimes it isn't until much later that the world understands their greatness.

What's that got to do with you? Check this out: *Visionaries are no different than you or me; they just turned everyone else's voice down in order to become great at listening to their own.* So stop expecting others to understand *your* dreams. They are yours for a reason! The best way to kill your dreams is to tell them to limited thinkers—to people who haven't ever felt what is in your heart. It's not their mission. It's yours. Don't let their fear become yours. Like Kobe said, "I never wanted to be the next Michael Jordan; I only want to be Kobe Bryant."

That is the true pathway to peace, my friend. Wherever those ideas of who you *should* be come from—your parents, your friends, a partner, whatever you're seeing out there in the world—get rid of them. You know you need to. I'm willing to bet they've been feeling uncomfortable for a minute now. Stop worrying about the approval of others. No more people-pleasing, please. Others are going to judge regardless. Forget them all. Make the right moves for yourself. *Demand your worth and walk into your greatness!*

WHEREVER THOSE IDEAS OF WHO YOU *SHOULD* BE COME FROM, GET RID OF THEM.

LOOK FOR YOUR WORTH WITHIN

Yo, Trent, you might be thinking, *I hear what you're saying, but how do I do that? How do I just make that shift to knowing and demanding my worth?* I feel you on that. I'll tell you how I did it.

I grew up in parts of the country where football was a very big deal. Y'all remember *Friday Night Lights*? That was my life. I was good at football, and I came to depend on it for happiness. It defined my worth. When I made the NFL, all my dreams came true. It seemed like all my worth was realized. What do you think happened when I got cut that final time? It's not rocket science. I lost myself. I lost my worth. I lost my peace. I went through a very difficult time in my life, but I'm supremely grateful for it now, because it gave me the opportunity to stop looking for my worth in the external world and look inside to find the true source of my strength.

The first step for you is figuring out who or what has any control over you. What's your version of football? Maybe it's current or past relationships, job status, bank account balance, how you did in school, or something else. Create some space in your life to make an honest examination, and don't expect this just to happen overnight. Try journaling or meditating or exercise, and don't just do it a handful of times. Create a real practice and devote yourself to it. You might want to find a good therapist to work with. I did all of these things, and they helped me immeasurably. A warning here, though. There are a million self-improvement programs and ideas out there these days. I've seen some people fall into the trap of thinking that they need to try them all, and that if they just hit upon the right one, it'll all be easy. Not true. The real work needs to come from within you. So don't get sucked in to the overwhelming amount of information out there. Figure out what you're drawn to, and don't overthink it. Make it simple, but make it happen.

Once you figure out what's controlling you, two things will happen. You'll see those outside forces for the lies they are. And you'll be able to separate them from what's real inside you. At that point, it just takes a conscientious effort to shift your energy from one to the other. One decision at a time. When a big choice arises, ask yourself: Is this in service to the real me, or is this for someone else? And then you'll know what to do.

Don't expect to get it right all the time. I don't—I still struggle with this from time to time, because I'm human just like you. But if you create that knowledge and awareness, you put yourself on the right path. It may twist sometimes, but you'll get there.

BE THE MAGNET

All right, y'all. We have been building up to this, and I'm ready to turn up the dial a few notches. You with me? Good. I want you to join me in becoming a magnet.

Let me explain.

When you don't know your worth, you have a void in your life, and you end up chasing something. Chasing happiness, chasing fulfillment, chasing money—whatever it is you think you need to fill that void. The problem is, the void comes from your lack of worth, and all that chasing just wears you out. Others sense the grasping energy in you and shy away, leaving you exhausted, lonely, and confused.

People in that situation aren't living their potential—they're just living *with* their potential. Living *with* your potential means that it isn't tapped. You're contenting yourself with what you *could* do, what you *would* do, if only this, if only that. There are millions of us living with untapped potential—the majority of us, I would argue. I had many friends coming up playing sports who had so much potential but never did anything with it. They never put in the work, never pushed themselves to let that potential come to life and see where it could truly take them. Living *with* potential, chasing *others'* ideas of worth—these are great ways to make sure the right opportunities don't come your way.

But once you connect with your worth, you stop chasing. You protect your energy and find your peace. This is living *in* your potential. Living *in* your potential means that you are on the path to being the greatest version of yourself that there is. It means fully utilizing the gifts that are inside you. Others can sense this, too, and they'll be drawn to connect with you. Your energy starts attracting what was meant for you, and this takes you even farther down that healing path. This is how you become a magnet.

Becoming the magnet in my own life has been one of the most transformative things I have done to separate myself from the pack and receive instead of chase. Being the magnet has allowed me to go on this journey without burning out and exhausting myself.

Where are you in your journey? Are you chasing or attracting? One way to measure this is by taking stock of your energy. Chasing is tiring. It's hard—way too hard. Some of us are working too hard. Working too hard to make people like us. Working too hard to impress others. Working too hard to be something we're not. Some of us are even working too hard to impact people. That may sound crazy, but if you are impacting people and losing yourself, it's not worth it. If you feel like you are trying too hard, I guarantee that you are.

On the other hand, when you tap into your worth, live in your potential, and stop chasing, something entirely different happens. Things get much easier. The people I know who have peace in their lives never chase. They attract. They're magnets, and I want you to be one, too.

MAGNETIZE ABUNDANCE

I see so many people trying to fill up their bios on their socials to impress people. But I've also come across many people with all the accolades who are still empty inside. Meanwhile, we often fail to realize that we are all already experts in one thing: life.

I'm an expert in life. So are you. I know that because you are still alive. I don't have to have a Ph.D. or be a best-selling author in order to do what I do. I can succeed because of what has already happened in my life, and because I've chosen to learn from it. My life has taught me far more than what any teacher in a classroom could teach me. I am by no means knocking education, so don't panic. All I'm saying is that you shouldn't disqualify yourself if you don't have extra letters after your name.

You're an expert in *you*. All your dreams, all your attempts, and—especially!—all your failures. Because failure is critical. It creates character. It makes the fruit of your successes taste better. And your ability to persevere through failure and learn from it becomes a secret power source you can use to help guide others. That's your own unique genius, and the more you get to know it and embrace it, the stronger your magnet will be.

I'm not just saying all this. I lived it. When I was chasing worth, I felt like people were dodging me. I couldn't find firm ground to stand upon. But then I accepted myself, grew my confidence, and found my worth, and all of a sudden I had a supercharged magnet on my hands. Things started falling into place. People I didn't even know started to gravitate toward me. Life became abundant because I had tapped into my own expertise, my own genius.

Once you're tapped in, you can shift from chasing and grasping to attracting and receiving—and then to *giving*. In my mind, this is one of the secrets to life. There are people with a lot of money who still live in a scarcity mindset, trying to get that next dollar and not giving anything back. Still always chasing. It's a trick of the ego, blindsiding them all the time, making them feel less-than because they don't have this, or they don't have that. Nice numbers on the bank statement, maybe, but poverty in the spirit and in the heart.

On the other hand, there are plenty of people who might be struggling financially but are actually wealthier than some of the "richest" people out there. Many of them are generous, living in peace, and living in kindness. They give, even when they lack, knowing they are living in abundance. They might not be giving money, but that's fine—there are plenty of other ways to give back and express generosity. No one can take that from them. Their true wealth comes from their connection with their worth. As I like to remind myself: *If I'm not wanting for anything, I have a better chance of receiving everything. It's hard to live in your ego when you live in generosity.*

A HUGE PART
IN BEING
THE MAGNET
IS SIMPLY
BEING. SIMPLY
KNOWING.
SIMPLY SERVING.

When we live in generosity toward the world, even toward ourselves, we start to live in abundance. When you develop the deep-down realization that you are peace, you are love, and you are happiness, you will attract all those things, both for yourself and for those around you. Each instance of it will make your magnet stronger and stronger. The good that you give as well as receive begins to multiply, bringing forth abundance. *Having the spirit of generosity is one of the deepest levels of freedom to be experienced.*

This is only possible, though, when you cut the strings of whatever puppet master is making you believe that you constantly need more. When you can do that, you are able to just *be*. When I'm in my best states of flow, I am just *being*. The messages from my heart just emerge, like they did when I was on those trail runs during the COVID-19 lockdowns. That's where the real power is. *Just being is so freeing.*

Whatever your methods are for finding that flow state of power for yourself, keep getting after it, and know that you're speaking, breathing, and living power right back into your own life.

"I am in my power," is my constant mental cue, especially when I'm on stage. It's a reminder that I am in my truth, I am in my being, and, yes, I am in my power.

Again, don't overcomplicate it. A huge part in being the magnet is simply being. Simply knowing. Simply serving. Be open to life, be generous, and serve. Stop scurrying around for the next guru, scheme, program, or whatever everyone else is doing. That's another way of looking to the external world for your answers. By all means, seek out help, but if you find that you're hopping from one thing to the next, searching for a magical cure, then you're not putting in the real work of making space to connect deeply to yourself.

Own all that is you, connect with it, and figure out what you need to keep moving toward your sense of acceptance, worth, and abundance. If you aren't in the best place, put in the work to get out. Maybe it's leaving a broken situation. Maybe it's finding some healing. Maybe you need to get on that grind for a minute. Maybe you need to fall back and be patient. We are all in different seasons that call for different actions.

Once I dove into the healing that I had owed myself for so long, I came to be in a healthier space. At this point in my life, I will continue to be who I am and walk through the doors meant for my life. I will attract the connections that are right for my life. I'm free from feeling that I have to be something I'm not. I don't have to do something that isn't pure to me. I don't have to belittle someone else to make myself seem more powerful. I don't have to use tactics to make people believe in me. I don't have to do any of these things because I know my worth—and I demand it!

Now it's your turn, my friend. Tune out all that outside noise. Accept who you are and step into your confidence. Find your worth, and you'll stop chasing and become the magnet. That's where true abundance lives. And best of all, when you get there, nobody will be able to take it away from you. Energy protected. Peace protected. Self accepted. Straight up.

Protect Your Peace Practice

Get real about your worth

I want to jump right into this one. I want you to first think of all the things that DO NOT define your worth as a human being. Examples are finances, status (relationship, jobs, social, and beyond), what you drive, where you live, your past, present, or future—the list goes on. List these out on a sheet of paper.

Now, I want you to grab a new piece of paper and start listing out what adds to your self-worth. For me, this list is very short: knowing that I was created by a great God. I could also include how I do my best to live in the truth, and many other reasons. I want you to get creative on why *you* are worthy.

Finally, when we discussed acceptance in this chapter, hopefully it made you think about your own past. Is there anything you have yet to accept? If you have found that thing, think about how you can work to accept and heal from the difficulty in your past, whatever that may be.

If you haven't identified it, chew on it and ask yourself once a day over the next week if there is anything from your past you have been unable to accept.

PART II

PROTECT YOUR MIND

TRUST YOUR VISION

*A vision is not just a picture of what could be;
it is an appeal to our better selves, a call to
become something more.*

— ROSABETH MOSS KANTER

I dedicated the first three chapters of this book to protecting your energy. Now we're going to step into what it takes to protect your mind. Before diving in, though, I want to say how happy I am that you've made it to this point in the book. I hope you're still locked in, and since you have made it this far, I believe that means you'll be here until the finish! I hope you are remembering to have fun with this. Some of these messages shoot from the hip on purpose, but I try to shed light, keep it real, and provide some humor as well. That's just me, y'all. So with that said, let's look into how to protect your mind.

Remember those opening chapters, when you learned to pay attention to and strip away all the things that were draining your energy? We're going to conduct a similar process here in the mind section. In this chapter, we're going to start with the necessity of trusting your *vision*. This also involves discussing who and what can shut that vision down, if you allow them to. Once you identify how this most often occurs, you'll be equipped to prevent anyone from killing the vision you are meant to receive and realize.

So strap in, and let's make sure that all that energy you protected in Part I will have a clear vision to work toward. I'll share what I know and what I've put into practice, and as always, I hope it may inspire you to develop your own strategies. I'm here for all of that, because seeking, refining, and trusting your vision is not a science—it's an *art*.

SHARING PRESCRIPTION LENSES

Whether you have allowed yourself to receive it or not, I believe God has given you a unique prescription for the vision of your life. To illustrate this point, consider going to the eye doctor (or ophthalmologist, in case you're wanting bigger words in this book). The doctor tests you to find the exact prescription to help you see clearly—a prescription that is, literally, for your eyes only. It's the same with God. The vision He gives you is yours and yours alone.

You might want those around you to be able to share the vision, which was planted in *your mind,* and see what *you* were meant to see. Vision validation is hard to come by. That was the case for me when I started trusting my vision of speaking, writing, and getting my message out. People thought I was crazy. I wasn't a speaker. I wasn't a writer. I was a football player. I wasn't supposed to be doing this—according to *them*. Here's what I learned: trying to explain the vision in *your* mind to others is like you putting your prescription glasses on them and expecting them to see as clearly as you do. What they get is discomfort, and a blurred-out reality.

So how are they going to respond? They'll probably tell you they can't see what you're trying to show them, or that your vision doesn't really make sense. They might even tell you that it isn't good for you or describe how you may fail. They can't see what you see, so they project *their* fear onto *you*. They put their impossibilities on your life. They hand you all their limitations and doubts, and if you don't know how to protect yourself, those projected fears cause you to lose sight of your dream. So then, instead of putting your glasses back on, you start to see life through different lenses—lenses that other people recommend, that look good on other people's lives. But you never get the same results. And the worst part is that if you let yourself digest those people's fear, you'll never put your own glasses on again. You'll miss out on your own vision and dreams forever. It breaks my heart when people put down the lenses meant for their life.

Let's take a minute and dive a bit deeper on this idea of the lenses that we see the world through. The way I look at it, there are three types:

The past lenses. These have you seeing life through your mistakes. Seeing life through your regrets. Seeing your present through a past that you can't change.

The pleasing lenses. We talked about people-pleasing tendencies back in Principle 3, and when I talk about wearing other people's lenses, that's what I'm talking about. Through the pleasing lenses, you see your life as all about impressing others. Trying to live up to the perception others have of you. Starting to see yourself as not enough, so you have to live a life of being something that you're not, just to get their validation.

The power lenses. These are the lenses you deserve to wear. The lenses where you see your greatness. The lenses that let you see the world as your playground, unapologetically, with everything working for you to create the greatest you. When I talk about putting your own glasses on, these are the lenses I want you to be seeing through. Go find them right now and put them on!

SHARE YOUR VISION CAUTIOUSLY

If you've connected with a vision that is meant for your life, I understand why you'd want to bring that to the world around you. But take it from me—this is the number-one reason why so many dreams are annihilated before they even have a chance to be born.

Know what the good news is, though? You don't have to let the failures of others affect your success. Don't let their limitations become yours. *Their fears shouldn't shape your faith.* One more time: Find your glasses and put them back on! And be careful not to share your vision with the wrong people. In fact, remember you don't have to share it openly with *anyone.* Share it by living it and leading the way, and leave the talking to others. Less announcements and more achievements.

Now, I'm not saying that you have to keep your vision entirely under wraps. Who among us couldn't use some support and encouragement? The key to protecting your vision is to be very select about whom you're asking to have your back. Do you see it as wise to share your dreams with those who aren't dreamers? To share visions with

GOD DIDN'T GIVE THEM THE VISION, SO STOP EXPECTING THEM TO SEE IT.

those who aren't visionaries? Why would you take advice on your vision from someone who quit on theirs?

If you do share your vision with anyone, make sure it's someone you trust. A proven source of support. Someone who not only has your back, but also has accomplished a level of success that your vision is hinting toward. How do you figure out ahead of time who these people are, though? I'm about to give you some tips.

There are two types of people who may project fear, doubt, and limitations onto your life: those who do it intentionally, a.k.a. haters, and those who do it unintentionally because they are trying to "protect you."

There's not much you can do about the first group, the haters. If someone's looking to tear you down, they'll tear you down for anything and everything. Win the Nobel Peace Prize, and they'll find something negative to say about it. You just have to tune them out entirely. Whatever it is you're trying to achieve, it's not for them.

The second group tends to be composed of friends, family, and others who have your best interests at heart (but really have no idea about the vision that has been put *in* your heart). We'll take a closer look at them in the next section of this chapter. Here, I'll just give you the bottom line, which is one of those hard truths I talked about right at the beginning of this book: Not everyone will understand what's been given to you, and you alone, to do in your life.

TOO-CLOSE BIAS

What I'm going to say next, many readers will find hard to believe. Others will be nodding their heads, like, "Yep, I see that all the time." It's something I like to call the "too-close bias." Here's what it means: the people you've grown up with—your friends, family, whoever is truly familiar with your life—may actually be at the top of the list of who *not* to share your dreams and visions with.

Think about it. Of course you'd be excited to share your dreams with the ones you care about most. I totally understand that, and I've been there. Imagine a few different scenarios with me here, though. Maybe you tell your parents about the vision you want to go after, only to hear them say, "Well, so much can go wrong. Maybe you should go the safer route." Or maybe you tell your friends, your homies, your day-ones. I remember when I told some of mine about the new direction I wanted to take, they just looked at me sideways and were like, "Okay . . . good luck with that." I sensed that they just saw me as the Trent they knew growing up, not the Trent I was becoming.

This touches on a fear I often talk about: the fear of the past. This can refer to the fear some people have that you are growing out of who you used to be and you may actually outgrow *them*. They may be afraid that they'll lose out on something they're getting from you if you outgrow your current situation and they don't choose to grow with you. Think about it: They are cut from the same cloth as you, but you suddenly start doing better. When you take off toward the stars, it can remind them of their own lack of growth. The fear of the past can also refer to something inside of you, too. Maybe you *like* some things about your past, and you're afraid of outgrowing that version of yourself as well as the people who were around you then. Any of this sound familiar?

The fact is, some people are just too close to you to see the greatness within you and how far you can truly take it. They are so blinded by the familiarity of who you are, or who you were, that they cannot see what you are meant to become. But nobody is an island, and we all need a little support now and then. So where is it supposed to come from, then, if not from the people closest to you?

One of the best things you can do with your vision is to bring it to the outside world—to those who are not yet close to you. When you step outside your close circle—away from those who are locked into a preconceived idea of who you are and what you're all about—you become that magnet that we discussed in the last chapter. You attract those who need your vision. You'll find people who identify with where you are coming from and identify with your message, and they will be the ones who end up benefiting from your vision. In turn, that loving energy is reciprocated back to you, creating greater good in the world. That's when *The Lion King* finally makes sense and you experience the circle of life. Cue the music!

Take a minute and think about your favorite restaurant—someplace local that's been there for you year after year, where you're a key part of the clientele keeping it open and thriving. Now let me ask you: Did you know the owner when you started going? Did you start going there as a favor to somebody? Maybe one reader in 100 will say yes, but for the other 99, the answer is no. The restaurant owners had to rely on two things for success: their ability to smoke a mean brisket, and the taste buds of complete strangers. If they had depended on their loved ones to carry out their vision, there'd be empty tables every night.

This happened to me, too. There were (and still are!) so many people who are close to me who never come to hear me speak or subscribe to my digital content. I heard *a lot* of crickets before I ever had anything close to a following, and for a long time, too! Trust me, no harsh feelings—the point of this chapter is that I now understand why that was.

NOBODY IS AN ISLAND, AND WE ALL NEED A LITTLE SUPPORT NOW AND THEN.

Now let me be clear about something. What I'm describing—this disconnect from those closest to you—doesn't apply across the board. Sometimes those close to you *will* support your dream, even if it seems crazy. My mom did that for me. She didn't see the vision of me speaking around the world, but she believed me when I told her that I was meant for more.

It might also be the case that you're married or in a close partnership, and you can't exactly change course and start striving in a new direction all of a sudden, all in secret. But if you share it, you might be afraid that your new vision will be met with something along the lines of, "I'm not sure if that makes sense for us or if we even have the time. We have to pay the bills that are due right now." If this is the case for you, my advice would be to put in the work to figure out how your vision can work with everyone's needs, and to lean on your openness and patience to have a real conversation and maintain your unity. Keep your respect for each other front and center and you'll find a way.

Finally, I'm going to ask you to put yourself on the other side of it. What if your spouse, or a close friend, or your child—young or grown—comes to you with a new vision, with excitement, with a dream and a gleam in their eyes? Unfortunately, there are many people out there who will unintentionally crush dreams because they just can't see them coming to fruition. They might mean well. They might be looking to protect their loved ones, but they end up dampening and diminishing their visions, forever.

If you are that parent, that spouse, that friend, please try to become more open-minded. Understand that what you want for them might not be best for them. Make room for their dreams and visions, and remember that everybody who ever achieved anything great was once in a position when their deeds were only far-off dreams. Even if you doubt that your friend or loved one will truly be able to achieve their dreams, know that they'll learn a great deal in the attempt.

And if you're someone who has had bad luck with sharing your visions with people too close to you or with those who were not meant to hear them, try becoming quieter and, rather than telling them, show them instead. Stop talking and start *creating*, but not for them—for yourself. On the list of people you're trying to prove things to, you should be at the top.

VISUALIZING AND CREATING THE HERO

Who was your biggest hero when you were growing up? What does the greatest hero look like in your eyes? Maybe it was a superhero, a firefighter, a coach, or someone else you knew who seemed larger than life. That's all fine when you're growing up, but at this point, I'm going to ask you to think about this a little bit differently. Okay, *a lot bit* differently. What I need you to know is that the most important hero in your life should be *you*. Figure this out, and it's an absolute game-changer, my friend.

As I've shared, I went through a long period after the NFL when I wasn't much of a hero, to myself or to anyone else. At times I felt lost, and I made decisions that were not in service of my greatest self. I was searching elsewhere for heroes, not understanding that I was becoming my own villain.

But then I realized I needed to make a change. Many changes, actually. I started out with small ones and kept at it, one message at a time, one listener at a time. There were days when I was selling my own T-shirts and advertising out of the trunk of my car. (Shout out to the few who were with me at that time—I remember you well!) Eventually things started to turn around, and I was no longer my own villain. I started becoming the person I needed to be. My decision-making now matched the person I was becoming. My sacrifices matched. My relentless work ethic matched. *I no longer had to search outside, and I began searching within.* I discovered that I was becoming *my own hero.*

Now, there are plenty of other people out there I admire a great deal. And I'm not trying to be a hero for anyone else—not even my own kids, because I practice what I preach all the way through, and I'm teaching them to be their own heroes. What I mean is that I'm not looking for a life template anywhere else. I'm just trying to be me. Remember from the last chapter what Kobe said about Michael Jordan? He looked up to MJ for sure, but Kobe only wanted to be Kobe.

All of this really hit me hard a little while back, on a trip to Las Vegas. During my wild times, Vegas always brought the wildest out of me. But on this last trip, I was in my hotel, and it was five in the morning, a time when in my earlier life I would just have been getting back to my room after shutting down the Strip. This time, though, I'd already had a good night of sleep and I'd gotten up for an early workout, and now I was ready to conquer the day. Right then, it clicked, and I just smiled. I saw myself as Nature Shells standing on the top of a mountain, cape flappin' in the wind. I was my own hero! Okay, let me stop. But for real, though—what happened in Vegas did not stay there. *I'm still living it, breathing it, and being it.*

Do you ever feel like greatness is meant for everyone else but not for you? That's a false narrative. Greatness is living and breathing inside of you begging to come out. When you put in the work to make this a reality, then you'll start feeling like your own hero. That's a distinct sign that you are living your vision as well. It's time to cape up!

I want you to take a moment right now. Don't think about your future goals or to-do lists. I want you to simply think about how far you have come. Even if you are not where you want to be yet, even if you're still struggling in some fashion, just think about how far you've come. That person you used to be may be a stranger to you now. If that hasn't happened yet, I know that since you decided to take the time to digest this book and humbly walk along this journey toward peace with me, the person you are now will be a stranger to you a year from now, in the best way possible. Every day, you're getting closer and closer to your greatest self. Be proud of that. It's heroic.

LIMITING BELIEFS

I gotta keep it real with you. When I started redirecting the course of my life and everything I knew, there were plenty of times when I thought it would just stay a dream. I had so many doubts. But everything changed when I recognized those doubts as *limiting beliefs*. I saw that I was putting limitations on my vision, hopes, and dreams. Telling myself what I couldn't be, what I couldn't do, and what I wasn't going to become. At the end of the day, I was even putting limitations on God. Holding back what He wanted my life to become. When I stripped away my limitations, He guided me to where I am today.

What limiting beliefs are you holding on to? How are you holding yourself back? If you are telling yourself that your visions are impossible, I want you to strip that from your mind right now. What God has for you no one can stop. Like I have said many times, *no hater can stop God's favor.*

Keeping it real, you may be thinking, *Easy for you to say, Trent, the NFL gave you this platform.* Or *Yeah, whatever. It's all just words.* I get it. I used to think the same way.

Let me address the NFL thing first. First, most NFL heads probably don't even remember who I was as a player. I spent a couple of years hopping around practice squads. I've got no rings, no Pro Bowl appearances. You didn't pick up this book because you remembered me from the cover of *Sports Illustrated!* Second, being a speaker was not a thing like it is now back when I got started. Like I said, I got rejected by platform after platform because of who I was, how I looked, how I spoke, and what I was trying to do. Whatever doubts you've got knocking around in your head, I promise you—I had them, too.

Well, now I'm still standing on the platform I created, by the grace of God, and with the help of some very special individuals who believed in me. It all started with my parents, telling me since I was four years old that I was destined for something great in life. They just knew it. My mom and my dad taught me to become my own hero. They laid the groundwork, and even though I was lost for a time, I was able to tap into that belief.

In the beginning, though, there was *plenty* of room for doubt. I'd be on stage for talks, with hardly anyone there. Sometimes I couldn't even get on stage. I made videos that no one shared or liked for what felt like forever. I lost people to whom I'd given my all. Through it all, though, I kept going, and only later did I realize that all along, I was becoming my own hero.

IF YOU'RE
NOT READY
TO EMBRACE
YOURSELF AS
YOUR OWN
HERO YET, MY
QUESTION FOR
YOU IS:
WHY NOT?

So if you're not ready to embrace yourself as your own hero yet, my first question for you is: Why not? You might still be searching for those heroes elsewhere, but why can't it be you? Why can't you be the one with the superpowers you're seeking from others? Why can't you be the one who changes the trajectory of generations to come? The one who changes the legacy for those who have come before you and will come after you? The one who shows that it's possible, creates hope, and creates generational wealth, whether internally or externally? Somebody is going to fill that spot. So why not you? What's so special about the next person? I'll tell you this much: Greatness is only achieved by those who have mastered their limiting beliefs. By those who have protected their vision from their own doubt.

THE GIFT OF UNANSWERED PRAYERS

You might be thinking, *Trent, man—I keep trying, but I keep getting rejected.* And I hear you on that. Some other time I'll tell you about all the different teams that cut me, and all the different ways I got cut. But here's what I really think about all that: Any place where you're getting rejected—that isn't the place for you. I believe rejection is a sign that you're meant for greater things.

When you do encounter rejection, pay attention. Some of us will keep trying to open a door that's meant to stay locked. Even if that door is attractive and leads to something you think you want in your life, there's a reason it's staying locked. It's the square peg/round hole situation. It just may not be what's meant for you, my friend.

For me, the locked door of the NFL is what led me to where I am. That locked door was the biggest blessing I have ever experienced. Just like my guy Garth Brooks said, "Some of God's greatest gifts are unanswered prayers." You wouldn't be reading this book if my NFL prayer had been answered. Did I understand this at the time when my NFL dreams were dying? No way. But I kept going, trusting God's understanding over my own.

You don't need me to tell you that many things aren't meant to work out. But what is meant to work out can and will. So I need you to keep going down that path, bouncing back after setbacks so you can get that reward at the end. Be your own hero and keep taking steps.

BE THE FINISHER

These days, people are great at starting things. But what's the point of starting something, let alone many things, if nothing gets finished? I hate to say it, but a lot of people, maybe even most, don't finish. I've talked about professional people-pleasers—well, a lot of people are professional quitters, too.

When I first tapped into my vision, I signed the contract with myself that I was going to finish. I knew it was meant for my life. There was going to be no deviating; I was sticking with it. Through thick and thin, ups and downs, losses and setbacks, new friends and lost friends, I was going to stay true to my vision. My mission was to go through it. I knew that *I would never get to it, if I didn't go through it.*

So many people are only *interested* in the vision. They are interested, and if they don't like the result right away, their lack of commitment leads them to jump to the next thing. I think of them as "disloyal gardeners." They plant a random seed here or there, day after day. But then they don't trust the process and put in the work after planting it—like watering, trimming, and nurturing the vision. Instead, when it doesn't turn into a harvest immediately, overnight, they think it's not meant for them, and they jump ship.

This tendency creates a lot of unfinished business. People die with unfinished business. That's one of my biggest fears and driving forces. I want to live my vision out to completion. I wanna die with a smile on my face, knowing I put in the work to complete the vision that was given to me.

This is exacerbated by all the distractions out there, such as everyone on social media making us think, *I should be doing this or that.* So we give this or that a try, but when we don't see instant success (support, followers, money, etc.), we quit on our vision. Microwave Generation–type stuff. Instant Gratification Syndrome. "Must not be for me" kind of talk. Then we end up putting on someone else's glasses again.

But know this: The bigger your dream is, the more likely others won't see it for you. You may be the first to create something huge. How could anyone else understand that before you actually take the steps to create and live in it? Be careful, though—don't expect a decade's worth of results after a month of work. Stick with it. Enjoy each step of the staircase instead of trying to scale the whole thing at once. The journey should be more enjoyable than the destination anyways.

If you truly want to protect your vision, stop abandoning it for the next flavor of the week. Stop cheating on your vision with a borrowed vision from someone else's life. That's the perfect recipe to live life incomplete. Know your true vision and don't let distractions knock you off your path. Be your own finisher.

YOU ARE THE HERO

Listen up: You already are a hero and you may not even realize it. One thing we all have in common is that we are overcomers. You are here, baby! I can't even imagine the obstacles that you had to overcome in order to get to this point in life. You have overcome the odds. Maybe it's family trauma, loss, doubt, setbacks, addiction, medical problems, life problems—you continue to endure and overcome it all! Even when you had to win ugly. You have overcome the statistics even though you may not see it yet. Everything you've been through has given you hero DNA. But it goes nowhere unless you recognize it and step into it. That's a you move. That person you've been searching for? That's you, hero. That person you are waiting on to make it happen for your life? That's you, hero. Claim it. Own it. Live it, hero.

Protect Your Peace Practice

Write a brief vision statement

Now that you recognize you are a hero, also recognize that what may be holding you back are limited beliefs. What are some of yours?

What is one step you can take toward overcoming those beliefs?

Now, taking the core values you identified in the exercise in Principle 1, how can you use those values in order to create a vision statement that can help you grow personally and/or professionally?

Vision Statement (cheat-codes): six to eight sentences. Include your values. What are you passionate about? What difference can you make? Short-term and long-term goals?

P.S.: Remember to be careful who you share your vision with (wink-wink). And once that vision becomes clear, don't trade your prescription for anyone else's.

GUARD YOUR FOCUS

The key to realizing a dream is to focus not on success but on significance.

— OPRAH WINFREY

Don't be discouraged if you are one of many who has not locked in on your vision just yet. Honestly, if you are doing everything you need to do to receive it, there may be a reason why it has not been revealed to you yet.

But I have some good news. Diving deep into finding and protecting your *focus* can help you if you need more clarity on your vision. On the flip side, if you already have an idea of what your vision is, improving your focus can help you bring your vision and goals to life. You see, what you focus on influences how you feel. How you feel influences your actions. Your actions provide your results. The root of that entire sequence is focus.

It pains me that most people guard their phone or social media accounts more closely than they do their focus. Fingerprints, face recognition, number codes—all just to get into a phone. Two-step verification to tap into social media. Most of us don't have those types of safeguards on our focus. One solid tool our phones do have is the "Do Not Disturb" mode. Sometimes we need to apply this mode to our *life*. Do not disturb my focus; do not disturb my mind. That's what we'll look at in this chapter.

DISTRACTION ENTERTAINMENT

So many of us are distracted by our phones, other types of technology, or something else that is preventing our lives from moving forward. Once we shed light on these distraction behaviors, what lessons will arise? Are you lacking presence, falling behind on your goals, or wasting precious time?

Guarding our focus is one of the biggest responsibilities we have as human beings. So many of us get off-track from who we are supposed to be because we are too skilled at entertaining distractions. We are *professionals* at indulging in distractions. Now, some distractions are fine—I've mentioned my love for my trail runs down here in the Texas wilderness. Sometimes when the demands of daily life feel a little too heavy, the distraction of some quiet time in nature is exactly what I need. For this discussion, I'm focusing on another type of distraction—the type that doesn't move you forward in a positive direction. The type that keeps you on autopilot. Those habits that keep you paralyzed in life and stuck in the average.

IF YOUR MIND
IS BEING
ENTERTAINED BY
DISTRACTIONS,
YOUR SOUL WILL
BE AS WELL.

When you let distractions rob you of your focus, I call it "doing random." Maybe it's scrolling through social media, playing a game on your phone . . . you fill in the blank. Doing random is focusing on distractions, rather than what needs to get done. When you are trying to accomplish something, don't do random. Doing random will keep you grounded in mediocrity. Doing random will lock you up in stress. Doing random will produce unwanted, random results.

Think about your typical weekday for a moment. Maybe you've got a lot going on: work, kids, school, whatever it may be. If you're truly showing up in these areas, you'll have a productive routine that keeps you from doing a whole lot of random. But what about your free time? Or what if you're between jobs, or looking to launch a new vision, like I was when my NFL career came to an end?

If you find too much of your time taken up with doing random, start small and build a routine. Plan the morning to get activated—go for a walk, journal, meditate, you fill in the blank. This will create some positive momentum to your day and get you headed in the right direction. Then end the day with another bookend routine that helps you wind down—controlled breathing, reading, or something similar. I personally love to do what I call "reflective therapy." I spend 10 minutes before I shut it down for the night reflecting on three things I appreciate from that day. A good night's sleep will make a big difference for the next day. You can't win your morning if you don't win your night. There are people who wake up with intention and control their day; there are others who wake up going wherever the wind blows them, allowing the day to control them. The difference is focus.

In my work, both with groups and with individuals, I like to ask, "Why are you living? What is the reason you live?" I've found that very few people have an answer to that. When we don't have an answer, we become very susceptible to distractions. The real problem is that whatever we feed our minds also grows in our souls. If your mind is being entertained by distractions, your soul will be as well. When this happens, you surrender your peace, you lose touch with your purpose, and you're left with stress, chaos, and confusion.

Is it an easy task to shift your focus from random distractions and center it on your vision? No, it sure isn't. We live in a world full of distractions, and the designers of those games on your phone and your social media apps are very knowledgeable about human psychology and the all the neurochemical mechanisms that keep you playing and posting. But once you're aware of this and accept that it's real, you then have the power to hit the reset button and change the course of your life. Does it happen overnight? No.

The change in your life will occur if you start to make small changes, one step at a time, until you improve your focus, are living out your vision, and bringing your greatness to the world as you were meant to. How do I know? I have lived both sides of the coin and am living, breathing proof that you can make one choice consistently that can lead to a whole new life.

As real as I can put it: Start starving distractions instead of entertaining them. Start feeding your focus by becoming more intentional with your life. Spend some time planning in the morning rather than scrolling. A distracted world creates distracted lives—break the chains!

The first step is to notice when distractions are taking over your focus. For most of us, it's going to be picking up that phone for no good reason, but for you it might be something else. Whatever it is, when it happens, take note. Catch yourself, and re-center your focus. I would suggest you create a short mantra for yourself to use in these moments, like "Here and now." Or perhaps, "Re-center, refocus." Whatever works for you! The more you start identifying when you become distracted and are able to reel yourself back in, the greater your overall focus will become. In meditation, this technique is known as "noting." You note that you were distracted, and this act alone helps bring you back to your focus.

Now here's a radical suggestion. You ready? *Put the phone away.* I do it all the time. I've told you about my sunrise routine, and I use that Do Not Disturb mode on the daily. Just put it away. Put it in a drawer somewhere, leave it in the car, whatever you need to do. If you need to have it nearby because you're waiting on a call, or you've got work or family responsibilities, I get it. Leave it in the next room, then. Heck, just putting it slightly out of reach will reduce the number of times you pick it up, and it'll give you that extra moment to catch yourself and re-center your focus.

SOLUTION-MINDED

Another big challenge to the protection of your mind and your peace is the tendency many of us have to focus on problems. Have you ever noticed how someone who constantly talks about problems is rarely the one to provide solid solutions? It's hard to focus on doing both at the same time.

The next time a problem arises for you, stop and notice what typically happens in your mind. Do you fixate on problems and complain about them? Or do you start thinking about solutions?

If you find yourself dwelling on a problem, notice the negative sensation you feel and allow that to be the spark that shifts you toward seeking a solution. It's better to think of whatever is standing before you as a *challenge*, rather than a *problem*. In cognitive psychology, this is called "re-framing." If you focus on the problem, you just see something standing in your way. If you can re-frame the problem and see it as a challenge instead, you shift the focus back to your path, your vision, and your progress. Rather than complaining about the road being closed, you can then say, "Okay, that wasn't exactly the right road. It's time to find another route to where I'm headed."

This can be hard—I get it. But are you making it harder for yourself than it needs to be? If you're someone who fixates on problems rather than solutions, then consider that maybe *you don't want to redirect your focus.* Maybe you're overwhelmed at the thought of throwing your energy and focus into doing what you know you need to do to make those visions become realities, and it's a lot easier and safer to focus on your problems and the reasons why you can't achieve your dreams.

Is this you? I know the truth may hurt, but even when it hurts, it always helps. Earlier I talked about the people I've come across who were content just sit in their potential and say, "I coulda done that." (Except *content* isn't the right word, because none of them were truly content. None of them were at peace.) So if you find yourself focusing on problems and feeling too overwhelmed to shift to solutions, help is out there. Maybe it's just a case of breaking things down into smaller steps and achieving one small thing at a time. Maybe the obstacle in your way is something bigger—and a mental health professional can help you figure that out.

Either way, the problems in your life are out of your control anyway, so why waste your focus on things over which you have no power? With a re-frame, your focus shifts from what's blocking you to what you need to do for yourself. It's the first step in taking the power back.

BEING PRESENT IS A PRESENT

How many of us are missing out on the beauty in life simply because we are not paying attention to the moments happening right in front of us? How many of us have our heads buried in our phones so much that we forget to look up? I literally tell people to *"Look up!"* Disconnect so you can be present with yourself and with your loved ones.

As I mentioned earlier, we live in a world full of distractions. Ads, apps, jobs, friends, family—you name it. Everything is after our attention. How often do we give our finite amount of energy and focus to things that truly don't matter? When we succumb to these distractions, negative moods and negative energy start to creep in. Let this go on too long, and the results are anxiety and depression.

Ancient wisdom tells us how those who are too focused on the past end up depressed, and those who are too focused on the future are filled with anxiety. When you are in the present moment, that is when you can achieve true peace. These ideas are largely credited to Lao Tzu, a Chinese philosopher who lived almost 3,000 years ago. Amazing how the message is so true even today; it's truly timeless.

I don't believe it's a coincidence that anxiety and depression are rising in the same age when screen time is at an all-time high. So many of us are stuck looking down at our screens that we are missing out on what really matters in life. Stop looking down at what seems to matter on a screen and look up at what truly matters.

Just the other day I was at my daughter Marlee's swim practice. I'm usually really big on not having my phone out in these situations, but I don't claim to be perfect. I picked up my phone once, and it was then that I felt her look at me. It was the one moment when she was trying to find Daddy to admire her killing it in the swim game, and I was distracted. I then did what I usually do and put my phone away. Right after that, I went to my go-to mental cue during these moments: *How can I be more present?* After all, I was only going to have this day, this moment *once*. One chance to be present in this moment with my daughter.

This goes not just for special events like swim meets, but also in our everyday interactions. Sometimes when it's time to get my kids off to school, I find myself thinking, "Man, it's too early!" But then I catch myself, and remind myself of how one day, they are going to be too cool to want me to take them to school. I'm close with my son Tristan right now, but there are things we used to do that he doesn't want to do anymore. I truly get it—he is growing up. Before long, he is going to be driving himself to school and an era will be over. I know I'll miss those moments, and I know they aren't coming back.

One thing I've noticed at all my kids' events is that the people most present were typically the grandparents. I think they realize how precious being present is. How you can't turn back the hands of time. Once you grow older and experience all the losses they have seen, you know more than anyone about the gift of life, the gift of presence, and how to appreciate what's in front of you.

DON'T MISS THE MOMENT

So when my kids ask me to come outside and play a game they've made up that makes absolutely no sense to me, I think: *Let's do it*. I know my son will be doing his own thing before too long. I know my little girls are going to be in middle school, then high school, on their way to becoming women and maybe having their own families one day, and these opportunities will be gone forever.

The more we have our heads down, the more we miss out on life. There is a mother out there who is missing her daughter's first steps because she's on her phone. There's a father somewhere who's missing his son score a touchdown because he is watching a football game on his phone.

How many of us are guilty of missing moments? Imagine if that was the last moment you had with that special person in your life, and you decided to spend it in distraction, instead of being present with them and yourself? That might seem a little extreme, but during the time I've been writing this book, I have lost more family members and loved ones than I am going to mention right now, so it's on my mind.

Listen, as real as I can put it: Moments turn into memories. And at some point, memories may be all we have. I'm blessed that I have been able to see a lot of my kids' milestones: their first words, first cartwheels, first lost teeth. I was able to experience these moments because I decided to look up and not be buried in distraction. I remind myself often: *This isn't going to last forever.* My kids being the age they are. Being in love with my wife.

BEING PRESENT IS A GIFT. A GIFT WE GIVE TO OTHERS. A GIFT WE GIVE TO OUR DREAMS.

Seemingly small moments multiply, generating wealth in my soul. When things go bad, I remind myself of the same thing: *This won't last forever.* Bad years, bad months, bad days, bad moments—they won't last, especially if I keep my focus on my dreams and vision.

Think about your own habits for a moment, as well as your daily interactions with your kids, your partner, and your loved ones. On a scale from 1 to 10, how present are you? Think about who matters most in your life. What would you want to do with them if they were gone? Go do it.

So many relationships fail because of a lack of focus. Kids are becoming more and more disconnected from their parents. Even in friendships disconnection has sadly become the norm. Undivided attention is most often the best gift you can give. When our focus is locked in during moments that truly matter, we lock back in to our peace, as our minds, bodies, and souls can literally feel that we are connected to what we are supposed to be connected to in that very moment.

I don't want you to get to the point in your life where you distracted yourself for so long that you are consumed by regret. I don't want you to get to a point at the end of your life where you realize that you have been *led by life, instead of leading the life you wanted.* The more that you can detach from distractions, the more you will be in the moment. When you learn how to be present, you start building up a *bank of wealth in your soul*, full of what truly matters most. Being present is a gift. A gift we give to others. A gift we give to our dreams. A gift we give to ourselves and our peace.

THE BATON

I am so grateful that my parents, grandparents, and those who came before me who positively influenced my life had a strong grip on their focus. That way, as they were running their race of life, they were preparing me either by example or teaching me how to focus on what truly matters. Having that was a gift before they passed the baton to me.

One of those key people was my mom, and as you know, I lost her while I was writing this book. When she passed, my grandmother said, "She just beat us goin' where we all gotta go." It was subtle, but it really warmed my heart and helped it all sink in. I may have gotten some of my competitiveness from my mother, as she always wanted to win—and she won in this way, too.

When those who have come before you—parents, grandparents, and mentors of all kinds—reach their finish line, they are going to hand that baton to you. Just like a relay race. That baton will be in your hands, and one day you will pass it on to others. The focus that you're bringing to the race of your life will not only impact your life, but the lives of all those who follow you as well.

My mother, my grandmother, and many other family members have run their race. Now I have the choice—right now in this moment, and in every moment—to decide if I am going to let my mom's race be in vain. Everything she sacrificed, everything she did for me and my brothers, big or small. Everything that she stood for. Everything that she hurt through, endured through, cried through, and prayed through. I could allow all of that to be in vain. There were times when I was tempted to use her passing as a reason, because I was so heartbroken, to stop running my race. There were times when I thought, *Man, I don't even want to do this anymore. My career, my community, none of it.*

The thing about life is this, though: The race doesn't stop. And furthermore, I know my mom, and the last thing she would have wanted me to do was to give up because I was in my pain over her passing. I thought about all that work that my grandma put in. I thought about my mom, my dad, and everyone else who came before me. Was I supposed to do nothing with that?

I had to realign my focus. I had to take a long look in the mirror. I finally said, "Trent, you better not let it stop with you. You got some kids that are depending on you, a community depending on you, and some people you don't even know yet that will be depending on you." You gotta cry it out, scream it out, whatever you gotta do. But you need to start focusing on what will bring joy and progress, not only to you but to those around you. I made that decision. I'm focused again. I'm running my race.

My mother and my father (who is still here and isn't going anywhere for a while) gave me and my brothers a big lead in life. I will be grateful for that until my last breath, and it's my goal to take that lead and keep building on it for my own kids. If you're a parent, an uncle, an aunt, a teacher, a coach—anybody who works with the younger generations—you've got the same opportunity. Focus on building that lead for them.

Unfortunately, so many parents don't make this same choice. In fact, many adults spend much of their time trying to recover from their own childhood because their parents didn't run their race as they should have. They allowed distractions to get the best of them. They allowed excuses to get the best of them. They allowed hard times to get the best of them. I see it all the time when I'm out there, talking to people, and it breaks my heart. When these people lose their focus and stop running their race before they are supposed to, they aren't even the ones who suffer the most. That falls to those who follow in their footsteps. The next person up. Those are the kids who have to run harder and catch up.

In a relay race, when the person behind you doesn't do their job and hand off the baton smoothly, you have to get outside your normal pace and try harder than everyone else to catch up. This is one of the places where *generational trauma* is born. People not running their race. Not healing from their wounds and therefore passing them on to those behind them. Right now, in this moment, you have a choice. The baton is in your hand. Your effort and focus will decide the lead or the setback you are going to provide for those who come next.

And this isn't just if you're a parent. Our influence extends to everybody around us, whether it's a friend, someone you are mentoring, a cousin, someone in your community, your neighbor, whoever it is. You should be digging as deep as you can, running your race to the best of your ability, so that you can one day pass that baton with a smile and give someone else the lead.

Or you can waste it. Play victim instead of victor. Choose to be stuck in your sad story. Choose distraction over intention. Set the people around you back. It's an option for all of us. I've had times in my life when I wasn't making progress, and that's why I am so passionate about this. What are you gonna do with the baton now that it's in your hand?

I want you to be someone who passes on that baton with your dreams realized, and minimal regrets. I feel it in my soul that this is one of the reasons you decided to go on this journey with me and why we're running this race of life together. By now you know, though, that it isn't going to be easy all the time. Like I said, my mom had a competitive streak that she passed on to me, and I rode that streak right to the top level of my sport. So if you and I are going to be relay race partners, I'm going to need you to run your race harder and faster than anyone who came before you. Both for yourself and for all those who will come after you.

Protect Your Peace Practice

Out with the old, in with the new

Take a moment to think about the part of this chapter where we talked about how *"Being present is a present."* What is something that is taking away from your ability to focus? (Spoiler alert: Consider doing a social media fast.) What is one step you can take toward eliminating (or at least pausing) something that is robbing you of your focus?

Now, with that extra space you've opened up, who or what deserves that extra level of focus? (Another spoiler: *you* do). What is one step you can take to shift your focus to an area in your life that needs elevation? By elevating your focus in this area, you will show up as a better version of yourself, *for* yourself as well as for those around you.

SHIFT YOUR PERSPECTIVE

The people who are crazy enough to think they can change the world are the ones who do.

— STEVE JOBS

The healthiest people in the world are those with the healthiest *perspective*. There are people in the world with cancer who have healthier perspectives than those who believe they have "everything." Others have a clean bill of health and apparent success on the outside, but poor intentions on the inside. When you realize you can have a healthy perspective even if you are dealt poor cards—whether an illness, the loss of a loved one, broken relationships, or something else—it puts you in a much better place than those who have been dealt great cards but have poor perspectives. Perhaps it's not surprising that those who go through something hard and then choose to heal often end up feeling more alive than those who appear to have never suffered major losses.

In the previous chapter, we talked about focus. Focus is an *action*—you choose where to put your energy and attention. Perspective, on the other hand, is a *feeling*—it's what comes about based on the interpretation or meaning you give to the things you focus on. People often discuss breakups in these terms, right? One person might look at the course of events and feel one way about it. At the same time, the other half of that broken relationship might reflect on those same events with very different feelings and beliefs. Your perspective plays a huge role in your relationship with the world. You have a choice of how to see things around you. Are you using the events in your life to live in your power, or is your perspective keeping you in prison?

Your perspective can be either your greatest strength or your greatest downfall. It's the window through which you see the world, as well as the story you tell yourself about yourself and the world around you. Those who have a *prison perspective* most likely have not owned their past, and thus they may be consumed by it through constant negative thoughts and habits. Conversely, those who have a *power perspective* have owned their past and committed to their healing, and now they use past difficulties as new-found strengths. What doesn't break you makes you, but only if you own it and choose to heal.

I have experienced both sides of this coin. I've had both a power perspective and a prison perspective. In fact, I often battle both in the same day. Once I notice my perspective is shifting toward the negative, I check myself, refocus, and get back to that power perspective. The strength for this comes from my understanding that I was created by a great God who intended for me to live in my power, not in my prison.

ACCEPT WHERE
YOU HAVE COME
FROM, WHERE YOU
ARE NOW, AND
MOVE FORWARD
AND GROW.
LET'S WALK THIS
HEALING JOURNEY
TOGETHER.

OWN IT

Wherever your strength comes from, the key to this shift is simple: *You must take ownership over your life.* Period! This is something I am super passionate about, because it's something that has changed my life. If you understand this, no amount of negativity, pain, hurt, depression, loss, setback, whatever it may be—none of this can control your life.

It all starts with you. Take ownership of your perspective and claim your power!

Let's go a step further here. Most of what has happened in your life has been a result of your decision-making. Your choices. No one else's. If you want to grow your life, it is absolutely necessary to take responsibility for all those choices. If you've been playing the blame-and-complain game, that is not time well spent, my friend. Has complaining ever helped you in any capacity? Helped you move forward or helped you heal? I sincerely doubt it. Accept where you have come from, where you are now, and move forward and grow. Let's walk this healing journey together.

The first step is acceptance. Accepting your current circumstances doesn't mean that they are permanent—it simply means that you're acknowledging your circumstances *and* you're taking ownership over your life. Taking control of your future. Otherwise, you're giving permission to your past—that person, that job, that loss, that depression, whatever it may be—to control you.

In order to grow, you have to give yourself permission to grow. This is only possible by owning it, whatever *it* may be—whatever is happening to you now, whatever is standing in your way. Once you do that, healing will begin, and it will create space within you to start putting in the work toward personal growth, whatever that may look like for you. Regardless of what has happened to you in the past, you are in control of how that experience affects your future. It's in your best interest to acknowledge it and work to understand it so that you can start moving forward in a healthier fashion.

PRISON OR POWER?

One thing we all have in common is that we all experience negative thoughts. Whenever I'm struggling with something, I already know that the negative thoughts are going to start pouring in. This starts early, too. Think back to when you were a kid and you skinned your knee or a friend stopped being friends with you. I don't know about you, but I remember thinking, "My life is over!" Or think about being a teenager and going through that first real breakup. Man, I know many of us have forgotten a lot from when we were young, but the feeling of that first breakup, the first time you were in love? That pain is real, and the thoughts that came afterward were, too.

It doesn't stop happening when we become adults. I was dealing with a torn Achilles tendon while I was writing this chapter, and when I was struggling through that first trail run once it started to heal, I found the negative thoughts pouring in. *Man, you aren't getting better. You're so out of shape. You used to be so much faster. You'll never get back there.*

And those are just the thoughts I remember, the ones that stormed into my consciousness. Who knows how many unconscious negative thoughts I've had, and how they've held me back in little ways? This is true for all of us. And when we don't notice negative thoughts and check them, we get used to them, and then they become a part of our daily life. Raise your hand if, when something doesn't go your way, the first thing that comes to mind is something negative about yourself. If someone walks out of your life, do you tell yourself you aren't good enough? If you aren't offered a job, do you assume there's something wrong with you?

I'm human, just like you, and I experience these doubts all the time. There is no mountain peak you can reach that makes you exempt from experiencing negative thoughts. What you can do, though, is start paying attention to them and shedding light on them, which will enable you to catch them before they catch you. Dr. Daniel Amen, a renowned psychiatrist and brain disorder specialist, does some great work in this area. Amen labels these thoughts *automatic negative thoughts* (ANTs). He suggests that when these thoughts arise, you should write them down. Then challenge their validity. Once you do simple exercises like this, you will see how untrue many of your negative thoughts are, and they will lose the weight they carry and start to dissipate.

Some of you have been around so much negativity that your perspective has become tainted. Sometimes it gets to the point where you want to tell your friends, family, social media, and the rest of the world just how bad things look. I've been there, and I feel for you. At the same time, though, enough is enough. I'm all for venting, but man, do you know how much this can multiply in your mind, the more you *choose* to stay stuck on it? When you tell yourself that you aren't worth anything, that your circumstances can't change, that your life is over—your mind finds ways to make that true. When you tell your mind, your soul, and your spirit that you aren't good enough, you automatically multiply all of that. *Prison perspective.*

You can only blame the negativity for so long, though. You may not be responsible for the pain, but you are responsible for your own healing. Once you make the shift, you will disrupt the pattern and create space for other, more positive messages. You can begin telling yourself how you were created for greatness. Take control of your mind and feed it positivity, and watch the positivity multiply. *Power perspective.*

So, you may be asking, how do I flip from a prison perspective to a power perspective? When my NFL dreams ended, I asked myself what it all meant, and I answered it with pure negativity. "This means that my life is over. This means there are no more better days in my life. This means I have no more significance in my life. My purpose is gone." I told myself that, over and over. I continued to find reasons to repeat that when I was stuck in that prison perspective.

But then I got sick and tired of all that. I shifted the question to "What is this *going* to mean?" When I flipped it like this, it changed my focus to the future, and I was able to see that leaving the NFL had given me the opportunity to find the true purpose of my life. Did I fully believe it the first time I said it? Not fully, but that's when I started to shift to a power perspective. I put down the tissues— not that there's anything wrong with crying!—and picked up that gym towel to start rehabbing my life back into the greatest version of myself. And that, as I shared earlier, was the start of RehabTime. I told myself, "This is going to mean that this next chapter is going to be greater than any chapter I have had thus far." I knew it was true, even if I had to win ugly at first. *You may not be in control of the experience, but you're always in control of the meaning you give the experience.*

CHOOSE TO HEAL

I can't stress enough how powerful it is to reject the prison perspective. How do I know? Because the foundation of all the strength in my life has been pain. The foundation of my success has been failure. The biggest setbacks can set up even bigger comebacks. When you ask yourself, "What is this going to mean?" you begin training your mind to seek and focus on solutions, rather than staying stuck in the problems. You begin seeing obstacles as opportunities to grow, rather than challenges that "should" be behind you.

When things don't go exactly as planned or as you'd hoped, train your mind to see this as feedback rather than failure. When I lost my mother as I was writing this book, people kept asking me how I could hold this mindset. Well, the truth is I did have a prison perspective for the first couple months after that loss. If I'd kept living like that I would've kept gaining weight, dug deeper into my negative thoughts, stayed in depression, and continued to lose myself. I finally had to stop and try to find the power in even *that* situation.

I'll be straight up: It's still hard. But I asked myself what it was all going to mean, and that turned off the faucet of the prison perspective and released the floodgates of the power perspective. I want to share this with you for an important reason. You see, healing doesn't always show up by itself. Time doesn't heal wounds automatically, despite the old saying. We have to spark that healing with our own intentional initiative.

How many times have you experienced something that was terrible in the moment but ended up leading you somewhere beautiful? How many of us have suffered a loss in our lives that seemed devastating in the moment, then ended up gaining something when it was all said and done? We've all been through so much in our lives, and although your pain might seem unique, there is always someone who has gone through something similar. If you haven't yet experienced any of the healing I have mentioned, you may need to *choose to heal*. And believe me, I am saying that with love. Making that choice is not easy, but ultimately it's easier than staying stuck in the pain. It was do-or-die for me. I had to make the choice and create the shift.

Is my healing finished? Absolutely not. Will I have to shift my perspective again? It's something I keep an eye on and assess every day. But I'm not rotting away anymore—I'm alive! If you are in a downfall or a struggle right now, this is meant for you. If you are in a rut, in a space with bad energy, and it seems impossible to make the choice to change, know that it's not impossible.

Flip the script by asking yourself this question: "What's it going to mean?" That's how you can move from your prison to your power. Move from "Why me?" to "Why not me?" This simple question can change your life. I know because it changed mine. My friend, you are ready for it.

THE DISRUPTOR

Let's wrap up the discussion of the mind by addressing something we've all struggled with: *worry.*

We all worry, though some of us hide it better than others. But whether it's worrying about a past we can't change or worrying about a future we can't control, worry is poison to the mind and soul. Worry can drain your energy and keep you stuck in a place of complete inaction. We expend so much energy worrying about things we can't stop from happening, or things that never happen at all. Worry takes our focus and perspective away from graciously appreciating what we have and shifts it to the negativity we can't control.

I have a cue I use to overcome worry when I'm trying to come back mentally, emotionally, or physically: *It could be worse. It will get better.* The first part of the cue, "It could be worse," may not make you feel better about your current situation. Struggle is individual—what I struggle with may be easy for you, and vice versa. You may think you're going through the toughest time in your life, and maybe you are. But it's the second part of the cue that I want you to focus on today and moving forward: "It will get better." Meditate on that as you go through your days.

I could have said, "It can get better." To me, though, that's not operating in faith or operating in belief. Hope is great, but actually *believing it* creates more confidence and increases the odds of the thing you're hoping for happening. When we say the words, "It *will* get better," we operate with a whole new sauce in our step. Whatever it is you are worrying about, I want you to work on letting it go. I want you to know that holding on to it is just weakening your life. It's an invisible weight you don't need to carry.

Another thing that helps me personally with worry is prayer. In the Gospel of Luke, chapter 12, God tells us, "You cannot add time to your life by worrying about it." God also tells us that the burdens are His to carry, not ours. I want to remind you to give your burdens to the burden-carrier. It takes a lot of faith to do that, right? Actually, God tells us we just need our faith to be the size of a mustard seed. Remembering that truth helps me, and I hope it may help you.

WHATEVER IT IS YOU ARE WORRYING ABOUT, I WANT YOU TO WORK ON LETTING IT GO. IT'S A WEIGHT YOU DON'T NEED TO CARRY.

I am someone who is simply human, just like you. It may seem like I'm doing great, but I have my struggles. I try to wear them on my sleeve in hopes that my message may touch someone like you. Peeling back the curtain, my prayer for the past couple of weeks as I've been writing this chapter has been, "God, renew my mind, replenish my spirit." How many of us are programmed to operate under the same patterns, more often when they are unhealthy? "Renew my mind, replenish my spirit. Give me a disruptor." I had a moment last night saying those prayers, and after that, I felt God speak to my heart and say, "You be the Disruptor."

Today, I disrupted my life. I woke up early again, and I went on a walk because I finally could again. I meditated, I prayed, I stopped feeling sorry for myself. I recorded a podcast to share what I believe God is trying to work through me. I did something to break the unhealthy pattern of self-loathing that was becoming too familiar.

I decided to be the disruptor. The disruptor of negative thoughts. The disruptor of negative habits. The disruptor of negative patterns. The disruptor of the prison perspective. I may have to make that shift again tomorrow, because there will be plenty of other disruptions I will face that are out of my control.

Is your life going the way you want it to go? If so, that is wonderful. If not, or if you want to improve it even more, how can you be the disruptor in your life? I challenge you to practice letting go of the worry and the fear. Disrupt the pattern. Disrupt the routines that haven't produced growth. Disrupt the lifestyle that hasn't been purposeful or profitable for your soul. Whatever hasn't been progressing you toward where you want to go.

There are certain areas in my life that I don't negotiate for anyone: how I raise my kids, how I protect my peace, as well as my overall standards and values. All that has to remain non-negotiable for me. I will no longer continue with whatever or whoever is not progressing my life forward.

Still gonna keep it real with you. I find myself negotiating all the time. "Maybe I won't do my rehab for my leg in the morning—that can wait until later." This is one tiny example, but do you know how many other times this week that will lead to me negotiating with myself to get me away from progress?

The first step to combatting this is checking myself and making sure I'm not compromising my non-negotiables. Living the best life possible? Non-negotiable. Being around greater minds and mindsets? Non-negotiable. Protecting my peace? Definitely non-negotiable.

Those are some of mine. What are yours? There have to be certain places you can take a stand where you are not negotiating, period. How many times do we lessen ourselves to make others comfortable? Settling because we negotiated. Not living the life intended for us because we negotiated. This is where worry comes in. You start thinking about those non-negotiables coming under fire, and that's when you get that sick, anxious feeling. Protect the non-negotiables and you protect your peace. Protect them, and you transcend the pattern of staying *mediocre*. I want you to forget mediocre and be as great as you were created to be!

No one is born with strength automatically available. No one is born with a particular perspective—you build it over time. Looking for that power perspective is a choice to heal. Although natural disruptions in life can be powerful, one way or the other, it becomes even more powerful when we snatch the reins and create the disruption ourselves because we have had enough. Be the Disruptor.

"It will get better." You know what? I am *making it better.* Even if I can't feel or see it just yet. Once you shift your perspective this way, your mind will eventually catch up to it and allow the life you want to come to fruition. I need you to understand that, regardless of what you're going through.

God's plan for you is bigger than your understanding, anyone else's beliefs, or any expectations that have been put on you. God's purpose for you is greater than any loss or setback. I've always said this, and I want to remind you: *Just because the path isn't perfect doesn't mean the purpose of the path isn't.* Sometimes the path isn't perfect and isn't meant to be. Our paths are often meant to lead us into what we need—and that *is* perfect.

Whatever it is that is heavy on your heart, right now, just know, *God's got you.* And it *will* get better. God *will* give you the power to make it better if you choose to. Sometimes better doesn't look like the way you expected it to. Sometimes getting on the better path starts with renewing your mind and refreshing your soul.

Be the Disruptor in your own life. Be the rainbow in the rain. Be the light in the darkness. The Chinese philosopher Chuang-Tzu once said, "Just when the caterpillar thought the world was over, it became a butterfly." Don't quit. Keep going. Start disrupting your life for the better, my friend.

Protect Your Peace Practice

Power vs. prison

Even though I work on strengthening my perspective, it still ends up putting me in a prison at times. I've talked in this chapter about how this can be a daily battle.

I have areas where my perspective is strong and gives me power, and I have other areas that are more of a struggle. Wherever your perspective is strong, continue to strengthen that.

In this chapter, we also talked in depth about negative thoughts, which we all have in common. If there is an area in your life that you may feel a bit negative about, I want you to write it down. Maybe it's one area, or maybe there are multiple areas. Write them down.

Now, how can you, over the next several days or weeks, think about how to strengthen that area(s)? How can you adjust your perspective to turn it into a power rather than a prison?

I can already feel you being the Disruptor in your own life!

PART III

PROTECT YOUR SOUL

SIMPLIFY HAPPINESS

Happiness cannot be traveled to, owned, earned, worn, or consumed. Happiness is the spiritual experience of living every minute with love, grace, and gratitude.

— DENIS WAITLEY

My friend, we have arrived at the heart of our journey. We have navigated through the deep waters of protecting our energy in the first three chapters, scaled the heights of protecting our minds in the following three, and now we stand side by side at the most profound revelation of this trilogy—protecting our souls.

Take a moment to reconnect, to re-center, and to refocus. This final section is the pinnacle of our pursuit, and will demonstrate the fact that protecting our peace is not a luxury, but a necessity. If you are not ready, gently place this book aside and return to it when your heart is truly prepared.

In this chapter, I will unveil four powerful forces that, when I engage with them daily, propel my soul toward the creation of happiness. I call these four forces the "Fountain of Youth," for they have brought youthfulness to my soul and rejuvenation to my spirit. They were inspired by the fairy fountains in my favorite childhood video game, *The Legend of Zelda*, and they hold a deep meaning that resonates in my soul. In the game, the fairy fountains were more than just power-ups or tools to progress through the game; they were essential to the main character Link's journey in restoring peace to the land of Hyrule. They provided him with the strength and courage to face evil and protect the ones he loved. Similarly, the Fountain of Youth forces I'm going to describe are essential to your journey of protecting your soul and creating happiness in your life.

Though there is no hierarchy to the four forces, I often begin my day with *intentionality*, which I envision as a compass guiding you toward what you truly need in your life. *Creativity* is the bridge that links you to these needs and empowers you to act upon them. *Mobility* is the lifeblood of our existence, as movement influences our mood and, consequently, our energy. Finally, *spirituality* is the transcendent act of connecting with the divine within, a wellspring of peace that flows from realizing that you are more than your physical body.

The common thread running through these four principles is that they are all priceless. They are not something you can buy with money, but they are invaluable to your soul. It took a significant loss in my life for me to truly understand this. As I grieved for my mother, I found myself searching for comfort in her belongings. But what I ultimately found was that the true treasures she left behind were not physical items she left *for* me, but the intangible gifts she left *in* me: unconditional love, happiness, and life lessons. Embracing this truth allowed me to begin the healing process and to prioritize the things that truly matter in life: purpose over possessions. Possessions vanish, but purpose lives on forever. Possessions may bring temporary joy, but purpose is what gives our lives lasting meaning. My mother's purpose continues to live on through every family member who carries her legacy, and her teachings continue to impact the world around us. She died, but her purpose multiplied.

The losses I have endured in my life have been eye-opening, and they have forced me to confront the true meaning of happiness. When I lost my mother, then my grandmother, and then my mobility when I was injured, I was forced to discern which patterns in my life led to negativity and which patterns brought me joy. Through this process, I discovered these four transformative forces that have changed my life. By embracing them every day, I am taking control of my life and creating my own happiness, and I want the same for you.

INTENTIONALITY

I wholeheartedly believe that a fulfilling life begins, or is reignited, by living with intention. When I'm truly thriving, intentionality serves as the cornerstone of my daily existence. Before I acknowledged this truth, I was absent from the present moment, neglecting to chart the path required for me to live purposefully. Remember when I mentioned "doing random"? That was my life—random. When you let randomness dictate your life, you lose control. Sometimes "going with the flow" leads you astray from the direction you were meant to follow. There are times when you need to halt the flow and forge a new one, and that can only be achieved by embracing intentional living.

For me, it's essential to attack each day with a sense of purpose, generating purposeful soul momentum that sustains itself throughout the day. Every action you undertake should be deliberate and aligned with your ultimate purpose. It has been said, "How you do anything is how you do everything," signifying that even seemingly unrelated tasks are connected. Washing dishes with purpose and a plan mirrors the way you raise your children. I know it may seem like a surprising link, but it holds true. If you tackle a full sink with intention, the task becomes more manageable and efficient. On the other hand, randomness only breeds chaos.

If something in your life lacks purpose, free yourself from it. Is there a relationship that doesn't contribute positively to your life? Free yourself. A harmful habit? Release it. Wasting time on anything detrimental? Cut it loose. Continue this process until every aspect of your life becomes an intentional component of your greater purpose.

Each morning, I take a few moments to pen some bullet points outlining my desired accomplishments for the day. Once my intention is set, I remind myself to live it, breathe it, and be it—LBB it! Then, every night, I contemplate how the day unfolded, acknowledging successes and areas for improvement. This brief exercise generates significant outcomes. If you're as ready as you claimed at the beginning of this chapter, I encourage you to try it. Tomorrow, write your own bullet points, noting three primary tasks and intentions—such as kindness and peace— that you want to embody throughout the day.

When you initiate each day intentionally, you might not have a precise blueprint of what lies ahead, but you'll be far better equipped to handle it. While life's surprises

SOMETIMES "GOING WITH THE FLOW" LEADS YOU ASTRAY FROM THE DIRECTION YOU'RE MEANT TO FOLLOW.

are unpredictable, you can stack the deck in your favor before facing the unknown. This proactive approach makes you more resilient when unforeseen challenges emerge. A purposeful morning serves as life's ultimate cheat code, propelling you toward a day—and eventually, a life—filled with intention.

Recognizing forever comes with an expiration date, we must resist investing our precious moments in people, situations, and habits that waste our time. Here's one example of how I counteract this: I devise a game to infuse intention into my weightlifting sessions. I schedule my workout just before picking up my children from school. If I need to get them at 2 P.M., I begin exercising at 1 P.M. (My wife calls this a bad use of time, ha ha; I call it positive pressure; and my brain doctor, Dr. Daniel Amen, says it's how I'm wired and thinks it yields great results.) This narrow window forces me to stay focused, eliminating any distractions or delays. I extend this principle to other aspects of my life, ensuring that I am present, attentive, and punctual in all my endeavors. This connects to Parkinson's Law, which states that work expands to fill the time allocated for its completion. If you designate an hour for a 10-minute task, you'll inadvertently stretch the work to consume the full hour, wasting 50 precious minutes. If, instead, you approach each day with intention and purpose, you'll gain control over your time and energy, maximizing the potential of every moment.

CREATIVITY

One of the most vital aspects of our humanity is our ability to create. It allows us to express ourselves, to explore our innermost thoughts and emotions, and to tap into our evergreen potential. Without creativity, life can feel stagnant, unfulfilling, and lacking in purpose.

When we engage in some form of creative expression, it brings us fully into the present moment, allowing us to escape the negative thoughts, anxiety, and depression that can often plague us. For me, creativity brings a sense of joy and fulfillment that nothing else can replicate. When I am creating, I feel like I am tapping into my highest self—the most authentic expression of who I truly am.

My creative journey began when I launched Rehab-Time. I didn't know that it would become what it is today; I just started and kept going. I refused to let fear or self-doubt hold me back from expressing myself creatively. And as I persisted, it started to feel more and more natural.

I firmly believe that we are all descendants of the ultimate creator, God. He has given us the gift and the responsibility to create, and it is through this process we can tap into His divine wisdom and guidance. Being creative allows us to strengthen our imagination, our vision, and our intuition. It is a way of expressing our deepest selves and exploring the limitless potential that exists within us.

If you're feeling stuck or unfulfilled in your life, take a moment to reflect on your creative journey. Did you stop creating at some point and settle for something less than what you truly desire? Remember that what is not meant for your life can kill your creative spirit. But with each new day comes the opportunity to reignite that flame and bring more creativity into your life.

I challenge you to make creativity a priority in your life. It doesn't have to be a grand project or a masterpiece; it can be as simple as writing in a journal or freestyling in a sketchbook. Allow yourself the freedom to explore your innermost thoughts and emotions, and to express yourself in a way that feels authentic and true to who you are.

Your creativity is a unique, individualized force that need not mirror mine or anyone else's. It transcends traditional forms like writing novels or crafting masterpieces. Opportunities for creativity arise when you learn to recognize them. One of my cherished methods of creative expression is freestyle rapping. There's a magical connection when words come together, creating a beautiful flow that springs from the depths of my soul. I believe freestyling has been the driving force behind my genuine, "from the heart" speaking style that resonates with so many people. For you, it might be as straightforward as preparing a legendary meal for your children or inventing a creative way to make your bed. Or perhaps, it could involve penning your thoughts. The essence of your creativity knows no bounds, and I refuse to impose limitations on what it can signify for you.

As you create, your energy, intellect, and spirit flourish. Whenever I go live on social media, I sense a divine presence guiding my words. While I might begin with a specific message, creativity often seizes control. The experience is electrifying and life-affirming, and I believe others perceive the vulnerability in this artistic expression. I create daily—whether through podcasts, writing, or transforming routine tasks into games. Many of these creations remain unseen, such as my frequent journaling or private activities with my children that ground me in the present moment.

I urge you to explore your own creative outlets, avenues of expression that resonate with your inner being. Your soul craves this vitality that accompanies creation. Begin with the most modest expressions, whether in the form of writing, singing (I'll save you from my less-than-stellar vocals), or experimenting with movement.

Importantly, your creativity should align with your personal intentions. Once you achieve this harmony, you unlock the boundless potential of your soul's expression.

MOBILITY

Movement is a powerful force that can have an amazing impact on your mood, energy, and overall well-being. It's not just about physical mobility, but also mental mobility, which can be achieved through meditation, visualization, and other forms of mindful practice. Both physical and mental mobility have the ability to shift your perspective and physiology, providing a wealth of benefits for your mind, body, and soul.

For many of us, mobility looks different. It can be as simple as taking a walk, doing some stretches, or engaging in a full-blown marathon. It can be a form of meditation, yoga, or any other activity that combines physical and mental elements. The key is to break out of the monotony of daily life, to shift out of the inertia of the mundane.

As Sir Isaac Newton famously said, "An object in motion stays in motion." This is not just true in physics, but in our lives as well. When we stop moving, we stop giving our life what it needs. When we stand still, everything else will be at a standstill. We become stagnant, stuck, and our energy diminishes. Movement, on the other hand, leads to further movement. It opens up new avenues of thought and action, and allows us to tap into the creative potential within us.

Personally, I find that going to the gym is a great way to get into that mobility mindset. It allows me to change my environment and awaken my mind and soul. It shifts my perspective toward clarity and my soul toward peace, giving me everything I need to face the challenges of the day. When I started practicing yoga again as part of my Achilles recovery, I realized that my body was storing tension due to the lack of movement following the injury. But as I began to move again, my body slowly started to open up, releasing that tension and allowing me to connect with my innermost self once again. The mobility allowed my mind to open up as well, reconnecting me with what's truly important in my soul: peace and happiness.

I challenge you to take a deeper dive into your being and create intentional moments of mobility every day. This is not just about physical movement, but about tuning in to your mind, body, and spirit. Even if you have physical limitations, you have the power to open up your mind through meditation and visualization, and your body through stretching. Start by creating a sacred space in your day for mindful movement. Carve out time for this practice, even if it is just for a few minutes each day. In these moments, you can reflect on your thoughts, feelings, and physical sensations. Take a deep breath, and release any tension you may be holding in your body. Begin with simple stretches, gentle movements, or a short meditation or visualization. Take a few moments to connect with your breath, and then allow your body to flow into the movements that feel most natural for you. If you are physically limited, consider working with a professional to develop a routine that is safe and appropriate.

As you continue on this journey of mindful movement, approach it with a spirit of playfulness and curiosity. Allow yourself to explore new forms of movement and challenge yourself to try new things. Keep track of your progress, and celebrate your successes, no matter how small you think they may be. Remember that the benefits of mindful movement extend far beyond the physical. By tuning in to your body, you can gain a deeper understanding of your emotions and thoughts, and develop a greater sense of self-awareness. You can also tap into the creative potential within you, and discover new ways of expressing yourself through movement and meditation.

So, take a moment to reflect on the ways in which you can incorporate more mindful movement into your daily routine. Maybe you can take a walk in nature, practice yoga, or dance to your favorite music. Whatever it is, make it a priority, and allow yourself to fully immerse in the experience. Take note of how your body and mind respond, and allow yourself to feel grateful for the gift of movement and the ability to connect with yourself on a deeper level.

SPIRITUALITY

Do you ever question your purpose in life? Despite my strong faith, I find myself contemplating this frequently. When I do, I immerse myself in deep spiritual practices. One of my preferred methods is intermittent fasting, which has often helped me realign with my spirit and higher power. However, fasting isn't for everyone; I encourage you to research and consult a medical professional if you have any health concerns about trying it. Other ways I nourish my spirituality include studying scripture, meditating, and engaging in prayer, as I mentioned in the last chapter. Prayer, for me, is a two-way conversation with God, where I speak less and listen more.

Your spiritual practice might look similar or different, but the essential concept is to allocate time to nurture your spirit. The modern world can be draining, and without actively combatting these pressures, it could lead to your soul's depletion. I don't want that for you, as spiritual strength is the mainspring in reaching your full potential.

When my NFL dream ended, I felt disconnected from God, even experiencing thoughts of suicide. Reestablishing my connection with Him brought those thoughts to a halt. Regardless of your circumstances, view them as opportunities to realign with the divine. Reconnecting with your spirituality reminds you that you're not alone in bearing life's burdens.

My path to spiritual connection involves prayer and conversations with God. Yours might be different—maybe it's a quiet walk in nature, making use of the benefits mobility brings. Maybe it's meditation. Maybe it's taking just a few minutes to yourself, away from the world's demands. Maybe it's a heartfelt conversation with a trusted loved one or a therapist. Such healing dialogues require deep vulnerability and trust, which I consider a spiritual process. Are you applying these practices to your life? Their benefits await you as a reward for your commitment to healing. Why endure life's challenges without claiming your reward, my friend? Give yourself the time to reconnect with what you need to replenish your spirit. Your soul is calling for it, and it's time for you to respond.

MORNING MARLEE

One morning, as I lay in bed, I stumbled upon what I believe is the secret to happiness—simplicity. My two-year-old daughter, Marlee, burst into our bedroom at 6 A.M. She pressed the button to open our blinds, and the sun lit up our room. With an infectious grin, she announced, "It's morning! It's morning! It's morning!"

DO YOU REMEMBER PURE JOY? WHAT SIMPLE HAPPINESS HAVE YOU LET SLIP AWAY?

That moment, so pure and genuine, made me truly appreciate the sunrise, her smile, and her joy. And it gave rise to a concept I call "Morning Marlee." Although I was already seeing her every day, from then on, I began to observe her more closely, to truly savor her simple happiness. She delights in the smallest things, like playing with her Froot Loops, exploring the house, playing in dirt, or singing a cheerful bedtime song: "It's time to brush my teeth. It's time to brush my teeth." I thought about my six-year-old, Maya, and my 13-year-old, Tristan. I thought about myself, and it became clear that as we grow older, we complicate happiness. We stop paying attention to simple things, and start pinning our happiness on big things that only complicate our contentment. It's the disease of "The Next!"—the next success, the next promotion, the next amazing relationship, whatever it might be.

Ask yourself, when did your happiness become dependent on external factors, instead of the simple things that bring joy to your life? Your soul craves the effortless happiness of a child welcoming a new day. Do you remember such pure joy? What simple happiness have you let slip away? Is your soul really that different now, or have you just forgot to cherish the simple things in life that mean everything?

It's no surprise that in today's social media–driven world, so many of us are unhappy, depressed, or anxious. We set unrealistic expectations for happiness, making real happiness difficult to attain. We trade gratitude for comparison, leading us down a path of misery. The followers, likes, blue checkmarks, and possessions are illusions, unable to bring true happiness to our souls. We neglect to appreciate what we already have. We define ourselves by what we lack, and we program our minds to focus on what we are missing. We exhaust ourselves in pursuit of the unattainable, missing out on the simple joys all around us—joys that could have made us happy all along.

Some of the darkest times in my life occurred when I tried to live up to unattainable expectations. I chased after what others wanted, setting goals based on society's desires rather than my own heart. I lost myself trying to become who the world expected me to be, instead of embracing my own simple happiness. In my lowest moments, I lost sight of the simplicity of happiness, believing perfection was the key, only to discover that perfectionism stood in the way of true joy. I know I'm not alone. Many of us create complicated, external goals and pin our happiness to them. When we fail to achieve the impossible, we end up stuck and hurting, defined by what we lack. But happiness doesn't have to depend on impossible standards. Aim high, but find joy in each step along the way. Embrace the happiness found in the gift of a new day.

What simple joys are you overlooking? Playing games with my kids, family movie nights, and sharing laughter with my children are some of the things that genuinely make me happy. I still pursue my goals and dreams, but I've learned to prioritize what's truly important—cherishing the moments right in front of me that I will miss one day.

Will you continue to pin your happiness on complicated external factors, or will you choose to live with intention and embrace happiness today? If you focus on life's simple pleasures, your life will transform overnight. Stay consistent, and you'll achieve remarkable results. Recognize you are worth this change and the harvest will follow. Shift your perspective, and create your own happiness, rather than waiting for the world to bring it to you.

Your soul deserves it.

Protect Your Peace Practice

Give your soul what it's begging for

When I do my daily necessities to protect my soul and my peace, I feel most alive. I truly feel the struggle if I decide to skip tapping into these areas with myself. The four areas I try to focus on daily are: Intentionality, Creativity, Mobility, and Spirituality.

I am giving you space below to map out how you can either create or come back to something that allows you to strengthen each of these areas. Once you write your ideas out out, you can begin or start incorporating the practices until they become a daily routine. If you are looking for examples in each area, refer back to the respective sections in the chapter.

Intentionality –

_____

Creativity –

_____

Mobility –

_____

Spirituality –

_____

Bonus Question: What can you do each day and/or week to create simple happiness in your life?

_____

ALIGN INTERNALLY

Trusting our intuition often saves us from disaster.

— ANNE WILSON SCHAEF

Sometimes we have to get away from all of the AI (artificial intelligence) in the world in order to connect and/or reconnect with our IA (internal alignment). Becoming internally aligned—in harmony with your innermost self—is the byproduct of building trust with the internal drivers that help make up your soul. These guiding forces may be different for everyone, and they have been given many names: intuition, discernment, gut instinct, sixth sense, and what makes the most sense for me—the Holy Spirit.

We are fortunate to have such simple, innate features that can bring us inner peace and lead us toward fulfillment. Sometimes they can be so subtle, though, that we ignore them. This is why I've talked so much about unplugging and disconnecting, because it's critical to get to places where it's quiet enough to listen to your soul.

As I'm writing these words, I'm at my cabin in one of my favorite locations in the world, in Broken Bow, Oklahoma. This place is one of my sanctuaries of peace. Tucked away in the Ouachita National Forest, Broken Bow calms my soul. The rustling leaves, the whispering winds, and the canvas of brilliant stars provide true tranquility. This small, quiet town is my personal haven on earth, a place that protects my peace and recharges my life. It's simple, it's beautiful, and I'm thankful for it.

One of the things I've been reflecting on here is how the times when I've been most lost are when I was trusting what everyone else thought, in terms of making decisions for *my life*. When I learned to listen to, feel, and trust what was in my soul, I found myself again. When I shifted away from the NFL to becoming a speaker and entrepreneur, I struggled. It was hard to let go of football. It had been my identity since I was four, not to mention my career and the source of my income as an adult—and then suddenly it was gone.

Now, sometimes internal alignment gives you a *yes*, and other times it gives you a *no*. When I got that internal *no* to football, it was hard to hear it. I was down to my last $200 and my firstborn, Tristan, was a toddler. I had a family to provide for. The NFL wasn't happening for me, but I knew I could make a decent living in the sport somewhere else. But that *no* was clear, even though I had the pressure of fatherhood on me. I knew I had to step out of my comfort zone, and failure could not be an option.

Externally, no one understood my decision. I had no proof that it would work out, but my soul was telling me that my future was going to be better than I could imagine.

I had brief visions of myself speaking in Africa and across the world. I'm speaking straight facts when I tell you that many people in my life thought I was actually delusional. They said things like, "Trent, that makes no sense, you have no experience speaking. How are you going to do that in Africa?" But my soul was radiating and I knew it was the right decision, even though I was stepping into the unknown.

I started making very raw, unpolished videos, as I described earlier in the book, and they turned into RehabTime—because I had to rehab and figure out my life again. Even before leaving football I had done a few speaking engagements in schools and it had lit my soul on fire. I kept thinking, *this is it*. When I got on stage and opened up my soul to others, I would feel such a strong sense of peace that I knew it was my internal alignment. It was still hard, because nothing externally was telling me it was smart, but I knew I had to trust it.

This is where most people turn away from their internal alignment. They let the external pressures drown out that inner voice. How many times have you done this? Maybe you've stayed in a job or relationship too long. If so, you're not alone. So much of our world is addicted to external alignment—aligning with what bosses want, what friends want, and what our families want. So many of us talk ourselves out of internal alignment because the first thing we do is ignore what our soul is telling us. Instead, we search for validation from the outer world. We seek to feel credible, valued, and important in others' eyes.

So many of us have trouble trusting ourselves. We neglect our internal gifts when others don't understand them. Nothing in my outer life told me that my dreams, my purpose, were even remotely possible. There was no following or revenue in this space for me when I started. If I'd been looking for external validation at the time, I would have walked away. But I knew I was aligned internally, and I kept putting in the work until my vision came to life.

It works the other way, too—situations where everything is aligned externally, but deep down you know it's not right for you. Maybe it was a job where the title and pay were right, but the work didn't feel right. Maybe it was a relationship that looked good to everyone else, but behind closed doors it was a different story. These circumstances can be just as hard, because we have so many ways of overlooking that discomfort. We can even trick ourselves into feeling comfortable in the discomfort. We often stay in a known pain just because it's familiar, rather than seeking an unknown peace.

Don't get me wrong: I don't want you to beat yourself up. In fact, I want you to forgive yourself and anyone else you know in this situation for settling for something that might have looked good externally. Now, though, it's time for you to realize how many more options you have that will align internally, leading you toward inner peace and fulfillment.

BETTING ON YOURSELF

When your soul tells you that something is right, listen to it. Bet on yourself. Now, there's no guarantee you're going to win that bet. You could be wrong. You could fail. But it's far better to follow your soul and be wrong than to follow something outside yourself and be wrong. At least you'll learn something valuable about your own journey, which is much more useful than learning what happens if you chase other people's dreams.

GOD DOES NOT CALL THE QUALIFIED, HE QUALIFIES THE CALLED.

PROTECT YOUR PEACE

When I started all this, my soul told me, "This is it, you are meant to be the voice for this generation." Looking back, I can understand why some people thought I was delusional. I didn't have any qualifications. I had no track record, beyond a few times I'd spoken to school groups. But I knew I could depend on God's qualifications. There's a saying I love: "God does not call the qualified, He qualifies the called." That could have not been truer for me. Even when there was no evidence, I trusted His calling, and that this was right for me. To this day, I make most of my decisions based on the same discernment. My internal alignment. I don't get everything right every time, but I know I'm on the right path.

My hope for you is that you will shift to using your own internal alignment as well. If you look back on your life right now, I'm going to guess that some of the most beautiful things you've experienced came because you trusted. You trusted and you put yourself in position, by listening to your soul, to receive what was meant for your life. It all starts with that process of listening.

There is something inside of you that knows what's best for you. That same internal judgment usually signals when something is off as well. Have you ever been in a position where there is no clear evidence, and you can't explain it, but at the same time, you know things are going to work out? You can't put your finger on it, but you know it's for you. You have a certain peace, in the midst of chaos. The external circumstances have yet to align, but your soul is at rest knowing in due time it will happen. That's the feeling I want you to lean in to. It might not be comfortable at first. People might think you're delusional, like they did with me. But that sense, that feeling, is internal alignment trying to rise up; and the next time you feel that happen, I want you to get still and quiet, and really listen. Pay attention to the things that are pulling you one way and the things that are pulling you a different way. Where is the internal alignment, and where is the external alignment? In the next section, I'll share some strategies you can use to practice tuning in to what's coming from your soul, and what isn't.

INTERNAL STRATEGIES

There are several strategies I use to keep myself in internal alignment. Strategy #1 is to *converse with God*, mostly through prayer. If prayer is not for you, try becoming quiet and asking your soul what it needs. Going for walks, meditating, and doing breath work are a few other options that can help you find solitude and guide you toward your internal alignment. Prayer connects me to what God has for me, what the world has for me, and what I was created for. There is no right or wrong way to pray—it's personal. It can be elaborate or it can be simple. Sometimes I pause for two seconds just to say "thank you" in my head.

One of my go-to prayers is, "God, please give me the discernment for what is for me and what is not. Allow me the ability to be able to see through the perfection, the promises, the presentation, all of the external. Please give me peace in my soul to see clearly and make the right decisions in my life." That not only is a daily prayer for me, it is also my prayer for you, my friend. The ability to discern what is right for your life. If you want to strengthen your internal alignment, then pray daily, and ask God to strengthen that intuition. I believe your soul speaks, and I am praying that God will allow you to hear it so that you become internally aligned.

Strategy #2 is to *practice the pause.* For me this happens in moments of quiet reflection during which I look back over my past and think about what I've gotten right, and what I've gotten wrong. Now don't run off on me here! This ain't always easy, but your own decisions can hold so many lessons if you can set your ego aside and learn from them. When I hit that pause button, I think back to situations when I knew something was off but went along with it anyway. When this has been the case, I've almost always suffered. Meditating on those connections has made it easier for me to notice that uneasy feeling, and I'm quicker to foresee those bad outcomes, and more likely to dig deeper to find what's really in my soul. It works the other way, too. In those pauses I also celebrate my internally aligned decisions, and I note how the best things in my life came from them. For example, I often think about this one particular party I went to back in high school. I was having a great time, but then something in my gut just told me to leave. Later that night, one of my classmates ended up getting shot. I'm very grateful I listened to my intuition that night.

I've found journaling to be a very effective tool for making the most of these pauses, and I recommend you explore it, too. When you're facing a big decision, write down the pros and cons. Write down what the external pressures are, and write about what you're feeling in your soul. Take your time with this! Anyone who knows me knows that when I am presented with a big decision, I'm going to need some time in order to weigh it all out internally. I give myself plenty of time to review my past choices, the good and the bad. Take this same time for yourself, and then make your choices. When the results start to reveal themselves, look back in your journal and notice what drove your choices. Check your alignment, and use that information to help guide your next big decision.

Strategy #3 is to *check your peace*. This one seems like it should be simple, but as we've discussed, it's easy for many of us to skip over what we're feeling inside us when we're tempted by external factors. Here's what I want you to do. When you're contemplating your next major decision, get out your journal and write a brief description of the choice you're facing. Next, write down your level of peace. Use a 1 to 10 scale if it makes sense to you, or give yourself a letter grade. As you're contemplating your decision, I want you to stay very connected to your peace. This can be hard, since there are so many distractions and external pressures out there. Be prepared to take your time. When I need more time on big decisions, I get into my principles-of-peace bag. Sunrises, sunsets, time at my cabin, running, the gym, prayer, pausing . . . the list goes on. When making big decisions, do what you can to get away from the noise so you can listen to yourself. Be wise in your own eyes, even if that means being a fool in others', until they see what it brings you. Once you've made your decision—and have really committed to it—go back to your journal and give your peace another score. What changed? Did the score stay the same? Did it bring you more peace, or move you further away from it? Keep at it, and notice the patterns—it's all helping you find your way to alignment, step by step.

THE HARVEST

So now you are on a quest for internal alignment and you've got some strategies to help you tune out the external and tune in to what's really happening inside you. So everything is going to work out perfectly, right?

Wrong, unfortunately. Humans are imperfect and so much of our lives is trial and error. It is in that imperfection, however, that you can find the golden ticket if you take the time to know where you are coming from, where you are, and where you want to go. When you take that time, you start to realize there is a guiding light inside of you. The more time you spend tuning in to it, the easier finding it becomes. It's a process, and it will take some time and some wrong steps. It doesn't happen overnight.

And if you're working to build a new dream, that internal alignment is only the beginning, because typically, you're going to see that the internal and the external are out of step with each other. Take it from me. When I started all this, it wasn't easy for me to tune out the outside pressure and expectations and commit to what God had put on my heart. But I fought through everything and stayed the course, and now my internal has aligned with my external. I have the beautiful opportunity to share with the world what's really inside me. I'm still working on it, even now, but I am enjoying it more than ever.

If patience hasn't been one of your strengths, this is going to take some practice. You aren't alone—with each passing generation, we get more and more used to instant gratification, to entertainment in short bursts. When I was a kid, we used to go to the movies all the time. We'd wait in line, buy tickets, and sit in our seats until the feature was finished. Now everybody is on their phones, watching 20-second videos all day long. There are so many things vying for our attention that it gets more and more difficult to work on the big things over time.

BELIEVING A DOOR IS GOING TO OPEN FOR YOUR LIFE THAT MIGHT NOT EVEN EXIST YET. THAT'S REAL FAITH.

I had to do a lot of soul searching when I took those first few steps on my current journey. In that process, I connected to a memory of my grandpa, from when I was about eight years old. Back then, I had even less patience than I do today, but I'd go hang with my grandpa, back in Little Rock, Arkansas, where he taught me about what I now call the *gardener's mindset*.

My grandpa had an awesome garden, and I was so tripped out by the fact that he could just snap his fingers and make plants appear. I wanted to be just like him. So he took me outside, and we planted seeds together. A couple hours later, I went out to see the plants, but I found nothing. I ran back into the house.

"We did something wrong—there are no plants, Grandpa!"

He smiled, and said, "Trent, you have to be patient and trust the process."

About two hours later I figured I'd been plenty patient, so I went back and checked again. No plants. I said, "Grandpa, it's been four hours now. What's going on?"

He said, "Trent, just be patient and trust the process."

That time I managed to wait a whole day before checking and finding nothing, and my grandpa repeated his advice. I gave up and put the seeds out of my thoughts. A few months later, I was back home when a phone call came in from my grandpa. "Trent, guess what?" he said. "Those seeds we planted? It's now time for the harvest. You were patient and you trusted the process." We went back to Little Rock and I helped him pick the fresh green cabbage, ripe red tomatoes, and some of the largest lemons I've ever seen. Each fruit and vegetable was a vibrant representation of the slow process.

Learning the gardener's mindset helped teach me faith. It taught me how to see the unseen. Many of us have that backward—we think we need to see it before believing it. Faith and internal alignment are about believing it before you see it, though. Believing that your dreams will come to fruition and that the harvest will take place. Believing a door is going to open for your life that might not even exist yet. That's real faith. That type of unshakeable trust is what allowed me to trust the journey even when I couldn't understand the path. It's what allowed me to stick to my mission with conviction since 2009, despite the hard challenges along the way.

What about you? Are you being patient? Do you trust the process? If you are waiting only two hours, two days, two months, then don't expect a full harvest. Nothing is going to happen overnight. You've got to be ready for those trials and errors, and you've got to develop endurance to get yourself through the downturns and setbacks.

In order to keep going through all that, focus on your internal alignment first. Align with the seeds in your soul. Nurture and water them over time with consistency and discipline. Don't worry about the results. Instead, train yourself to become fulfilled by the process. The journey, not the destination. The work you're putting in, not the fruit that you will bear. Believe you are growing, even when you can't yet see the growth that is taking place. Then, you, my friend, will be ready to reap the harvest. I have complete faith in you. Just like my grandpa, I know what's taking place below the surface and I trust the process.

Protect Your Peace Practice

How close are you with you?

I want you to first think about your internal alignment, or lack thereof. I am guessing that after reading this chapter, you may have a pretty good idea on whether you are aligned internally or not. I also hope that if you did the exercise at the end of Principle 7, that will help you align from within once again. (And if you didn't do it, there is still time!)

Just like our vehicles get out of alignment over time, as life continues to move, we can become out of alignment with ourselves. Go back and take a look at the *Internal Strategies* section of this chapter. There, I discuss my top strategies for getting back into alignment, as well as several different examples that I hope you can relate to.

Your choice: You can do the exercise within that section about making significant decisions (if you are facing a big decision right now, this is perfect!). Or you can review all my strategies and examples and allow your soul to come up with your own specific ways to internally align that you can practice often.

LIVE IN FULFILLMENT

*If you look to others for fulfillment, you will
never be truly fulfilled.*

— LAO TZU

Fulfillment is essentially an internal duty, something
we owe to ourselves. That said, it is part of that duty to
recognize and get clear on what matters to us externally.
One of the most interesting parallels I have drawn from
the journey of protecting my peace is how living in internal alignment has also led to external alignment, and an
increasingly fulfilling life. When I have peace, I am fulfilled; and when I am fulfilled, I have peace. When I lose
one, I lose the other as well. This has led me to create what
I call *the art of fulfillment,* which is a formula that leads to a
fulfilled life. It's simple: *Time, divided by what matters most,
equals fulfillment.* In other words, spend your time doing
what matters most to you, and you will gain fulfillment.

The first step, then, is to figure out what those meaningful things are. If you need some inspiration, ask yourself this simple yet life-changing question about whatever it is you're considering: "If I lost this thing, how would my life change?" If losing it would forever create a void in your life, then you know immediately that it goes in the "matters the most" category. Pause, think about it, and make a bulleted list on a sheet of paper of who and what matters most in your life.

Once you've made that list, I want you to go through it and write 1, 2, or 3 next to each meaningful thing. A 3 means you spend most of your time on it, and a 1 means it gets the least amount of your time. Keep this list handy and refer to it as needed as you read this chapter.

CHOOSE WHAT MATTERS

I have asked this question many times on stage. I say to the audience, "How many of you want a million dollars?" Of course, everyone raises their hand. Then, I follow that up with another question: "How many of you would still take that million dollars if it meant that you had to completely give up your peace?" All the hands go back down at that point. External gains—like a million-dollar lottery win—don't provide fulfillment. You can have everything, but without peace, it means nothing.

Peace is the number one currency in the world. So many of us overlook this, because it's so easy to fixate on what we don't have. "If only I had this or that," we say. "If only . . ." Well, I've had this and I've had that. I've had money and achievements without peace, and it was unfulfilling. I've also had peace in times when I didn't have much money, and I'd choose that any day of the week.

Jim Carrey struck something deep when he said, "Everyone should get rich and famous and do everything they ever dreamed of, so they can see it's not the answer." There's a long, sad list of people who illustrate this: Robin Williams, Michael Jackson, Prince, Anthony Bourdain . . . people who seemed to have everything *but* peace. Personally, I lost a great friend, my college roommate, to suicide. I can't speak to what was truly happening in his, or anyone else's, soul—none of us can. But I do know that we live in a society that has many of us looking in the wrong places for fulfillment.

Once I spoke at a high-level real estate conference. I asked the audience for a show of hands from anyone who was struggling with fulfillment, and I called on one gentleman who looked like he was ready to share.

"How are you doing in your life right now, bro?" I asked him.

He responded, "I'm doing great. I'm a top-level exec and have everything that I want."

"Why aren't you fulfilled, then?" I asked.

"I just feel like something is missing in my soul," he said.

"I'm sorry to hear that, my friend," I said. "Let me ask you something else. Who are the most important people in your life?"

Without hesitation, he said, "My daughter."

"On a one-to-three scale, how important is she to you?"

"Three, no doubt."

"Right," I said. "So on a one-to-three scale, how much time are you spending with her?"

His face went still, and I could see the heaviness on him. He looked stricken, and I had to ask him again. Finally, quietly, he said, "One."

I gave it a minute, and then I told him about my formula. I asked him more questions and found that he was spending about 80 percent of his time working. The time he was spending with his daughter was badly misaligned with her importance, and he was badly unfulfilled. No matter how successful you might appear in terms of money, status, the car you drive, et cetera, if you aren't doing things that are nourishing to your soul—doing what you love with the people you love—you're going to feel a great void.

LEARNING FROM LOSS

This lesson hit me in a big way a couple of years before I wrote this book, over the course of two very difficult back-to-back events that came right during the height of COVID-19, when we were all struggling with so much already. My mom, God rest her soul, was in a hospice bed, and because of safety precautions, I couldn't see her as often as I wanted to. It broke my heart—she'd been bed-bound for months, with sores that were like bullet holes. Even in the midst of her pain, though, she still had unconditional praise for life and for her family. Her own fulfillment came in large part from her unconditional faith, which was intact despite all she was going through. I remember being in awe of her strength at the time, but thinking about it now, it doesn't surprise me anymore. She'd made up her mind a long time ago about how she was going to live her life: She was going to work with my dad to raise strong children and have a strong family. She was going to set an example by being right with herself and with God. Well, she accomplished all that, and then some. Her teachings live on, and remain as the glue that keeps us all together. I cannot imagine

IF YOU'RE IN
A SEASON OF
DARKNESS RIGHT
NOW, IT MAY BE
HARD TO SEE
THE LIGHT. BE
PATIENT WITH
THE PROCESS.

having the peace and fulfillment I do now without having faith in the One who created me.

In those final months I remember sitting by her bedside and holding her hand. I wanted to cry, but there was so much joy in her eyes still. She was closer to God than ever, and I could see the light of her soul shining through her eyes, even when she could barely breathe. She knew exactly what she needed to be fulfilled, and she taught me and my brothers by doing what she loved with the people she loved.

Just two days after my mom's fight ended and she transitioned, a second event occurred that brought the lesson of fulfillment into even sharper focus. My daughter Maya had been playing outside with some neighborhood kids when one of the kids came running to our door and told us that Maya was hurt. At first, we assumed it was a normal thing—a knee scrape, a banged-up elbow, the usual kind of boo-boos kids get all the time. As I drew closer to where Maya had been playing, I heard a woman start screaming. I started to sprint. It felt like it took me forever to reach my baby girl, who was lying on the ground, bleeding from her head, going in and out of consciousness. She'd been hit by a big rock that was slung at her from a lawn mower.

We rushed her to the hospital, and she went directly into the ICU. There were more people than I could count working on her, and in the midst of it, the chaplain appeared. I started to think the worst, but then I was like, *Nah, this can't be it. I have to keep my faith.* After the scans came in, they told us she had some swelling in her brain. They were going to keep her in the ICU and do everything they could for her.

In the same week my mom had passed, my heart was now shattering in another way. I remember thinking,

Nothing else matters. I just want my baby girl to be okay. I said a prayer to God: "Take it all away, just don't take my baby away." Days went by. I prepared myself to miss my mom's funeral. Steadfast prayer, all day, every day. After four days, the neurologist came to see us with a shocked look on her face. "I have never seen anything like this before," she said. "She has made a miraculous turn and has healed to the point where I am not really able to see the injury at all anymore." That came as a massive relief, of course, but the season wasn't done with me yet. Just two weeks later, my grandmother passed. The lessons were coming hard and fast.

After losing my mom and grandmother and thinking about what it would have been like to lose Maya, it became clearer to me than ever that the people I love are the most important things in my life, and my real source of fulfillment. I took a look at how I was spending my time and made adjustments to make sure I was racking up as many memories as possible with those I love most. I consider this intentionality to be a gift from my daughter, my mom, my grandma, and everyone else I cherish. Those difficult months were darkness before the dawn.

That helplessness I felt—while my mom was in hospice, and while my daughter was in the ICU—made me think about the things I would give up in a millisecond in order to preserve what I cared about the most. I would happily give away money, significance, status, even my own life, if it meant saving the ones that I love. I know there are very few people who would say they feel differently, and yet, so many of us spend more time bingeing shows, working jobs, or focusing on distractions than we do spending quality time with our loved ones. And we still wonder why we aren't fulfilled.

That season forced me to change the way I operate. Prior to that, I would have said I had an understanding of what was valuable in my life. I never would have thought that I valued my business over my family, but when I looked back, I could see that my values were misaligned with how I had spent my time during much of my past. I had to really take a look at my time and how I was spending it, and my new intentionality has led me to consistent fulfillment.

I don't want you to have to go through all of what I did to share the same awakening. If you identified with that audience member at the real estate conference, then make a change, right now and going forward, for good. And when you do start to figure out your specific formula for fulfillment, whether you use the lessons throughout this book to get there or not, I encourage you to use your own specific gifts. Know what they are, embrace them, and share them with others, and you'll help those people along their path toward fulfillment and overall peace. You don't need to be a public speaker like me, but you can make a difference in the lives of others by uncovering, strengthening, and sharing what is uniquely yours.

And if you're in a season of darkness yourself right now, you know I get you. I've been there, as you've seen. It may be hard to see the light right now, but be patient with the process.

My most painful times led me to hone some of my gifts and taught me the importance of sharing them with the world. Even if you share your gifts with just one person, that may be enough, and may change their life without you even knowing. Make these changes, and make yourself an example of fulfillment, like my dear mom did. This is how to live in rejoice, rather than in regret.

ENOUGH

All this talk of changing people's lives might come across as a lot. Maybe you're having some trouble visualizing how you could have that kind of impact. Maybe you feel like you're not enough. You don't have enough talent to make an impact. You don't have enough strength to make a comeback. You don't have enough experience to be credible. I can't tell you how many times I've heard this over the years. "Trent," people will say, "I just don't feel like I am enough." And then I ask them what their definition of *enough* is. Believe it or not, I rarely get an answer. So that's where we're going to start.

Your first task is to define what *enough* means to you. I get away from it sometimes, but my goal is to remember that it's *enough* to have life. To wake up, have breath, have limbs, be able to see, hear, and taste. To be able to hurt, heal, and love. To be able to grieve, which is the flip side of deep love.

What is it for you? What do you want or need from life? Do you know? You would be shocked at the number of people who don't know the answer to that question. There should be classes in school that encourage people to focus on that question alone. If you don't know what you want, how could you ever have enough, or be enough?

I suggest you pull out a sheet of paper and define your *enough* right now if you haven't already. What needs to occur for you to *be enough*? What needs to occur for you to *have enough*? What are you passionate about? I challenge you to exercise those passions—as a hobby, at minimum, and as a career if and when you are able to. Do what makes you proud. I challenge you to use your alone time to strategize about how you can work smarter, rather than harder.

And take some of that quiet time to really tune in to what your soul might be saying to you right now.

To deepen this exercise, I urge you to identify what you no longer wish to tolerate. Having set your ceiling of enough, it's crucial to determine your floor of enough— what you won't settle for. This balance forms a contentment zone between striving for the optimal and refusing the unacceptable. This will steer you away from unhealthy ambitions, and stop you from accepting less than your due. Pinpointing my enoughs helped me cultivate a steady state of peace and fulfillment. Please remember to revisit and refine these limits as you grow and change. As you better understand your needs, your enoughs may shift.

PASS IT ON

Fulfillment is different for everyone, but spending time doing what matters most with those who matter most is a central theme for me. That can mean quality time with family, providing service for others, or anything that makes my soul feel alive. Not serving others for clout, or for notoriety, but to help fight for what's good in the world, helping others, while filling my own cup at the same time. I can go to sleep at night knowing that no matter what external things did or didn't happen, no matter what's happening in terms of money or popularity, I know that I am striving to make this world a better place. I know that I have made others feel heard, felt, seen, and valued, and that gives me a sense of value and fulfillment right back. Every single day. And there is no greater feeling than that.

I've been working for years to create ways to do this, and I've had some good luck, too, but if you're new to this, don't worry—you don't need much to start. At the

EVERYTHING YOU'RE GOING THROUGH WILL SOON TURN INTO EVERYTHING YOU MADE IT THROUGH.

beginning of each day, simply ask yourself a few questions. First, ask yourself, "How can I make myself better?" I put this first because you can't start to fill someone else's cup if yours is empty. You need charged batteries if you're going to shine. The answer to this could be as simple as a five-minute walk, or a few minutes of meditation. Next, ask yourself, "How can I make someone else's day better?" This could be a smile or some extra kindness at some point in your day. Finally, ask, "How can I make the world better?" This could be anything from being a little more diligent about recycling to a creek clean-up to curing cancer—everyone has something to offer!

Then, at the end of the day, ask those questions in reverse. Did you make yourself better? Did you better someone else's life? Did you make the world a better place? (Here's a hint: Taking care of the first and second questions automatically takes care of the third.)

If you're still struggling to visualize the impact you can have on the world, consider this: One way or another, you are already contributing something. You affect everyone you come into contact with, even in the smallest of interactions. If you're not working toward fulfillment or going about your days with intention, then you could be contributing something negative. You could be contributing to the demise of something. Contributing to the stagnation of something. Contributing to the regression of something. You *already* have an impact, whether you know it or not.

My challenge and wish for you is that you will take the opportunity to make an intentional, positive contribution to the world. Try out my morning affirmation: "I'm contributing something to myself, to someone else, and to this world to make it at least a little better." Remember, the things that are simple and free can often be very powerful. Contribute kindness. Contribute goodness. Find a way to be of service, and this will lead you down the path of creating and sustaining your own fulfillment. This will keep your fire burning, for yourself, and for others! Be an example, like my mom. It's one of the greatest medicines for the soul. *It's hard to feel empty when you are busy showing others how to feel full.*

Protect Your Peace Practice

A formula for fulfillment

I know you have worked your behind off, putting in the work to protect your peace in order to get to this point in the book! So I want to keep this practice super simple.

You can go back and do the exercise from the beginning of this chapter again, where you made a list of what's most meaningful to you. Think about prioritizing your life choices by putting into practice my definition: *Time, divided by what matters most, equals fulfillment*

Or you can simplify it even more. Take out a sheet of paper and put a line horizontally down the center of it. Label the left side *What Matters Most?* Label the right side *Who Matters Most?*

What would your life look like if you combined both sides?

Try to do that in the near future, my friend, and think about how you can be consistent with doing so going forward. This will help you figure out how to get back to doing what matters most, with who matters most, and living in fulfillment.

CONCLUSION

Protect Your Life

*It's never too late to be whoever you want
to be. I hope you live a life you're proud of,
and if you find that you're not, I hope you
have the strength to start all over again.*

— FROM *THE CURIOUS CASE
OF BENJAMIN BUTTON*

As we reach the final pages of this book, I want you to
know that this is not an ending, but rather a beautiful new
beginning. I don't know about you, but I feel full. Full of
peace, full of joy, full of excitement for you. I feel as if I just
had the most meaningful conversation with a really close
friend. I want you to know that I haven't just shared pieces
of my life to fill pages. I've shared them as compasses, as
guideposts, in hope that they might light your path and
strengthen your spirit. Life has been my harshest teacher
and my most compassionate friend. I've endured constant
battles in order to understand the value of peace, and now
I'm committed to spreading this message to every soul I'm
called to reach.

Let's take a quick jog through and highlight some of the truths within the chapters that have led us to this stage of the game.

PROTECT YOUR ENERGY

- **Principle 1: Set Boundaries** — The first chapter was all about *boundaries*. Understanding the power of *no* and how that word can be a complete response. The addition of external and internal boundaries can lead to the subtraction of stress and chaos. Boundaries should be bridges, not walls (unless those are necessary). And they can be bridges that lead to healthier relationships as well as peace.

- **Principle 2: Disconnect Often** — The second chapter discussed the importance of checking your *connections* and the power of unplugging and disconnecting often. We had a discussion about the power of environments, positive and/or negative, with some nature talk as well. Energy can be seen as an expense and a reminder of how we are all on a running clock. What you are connected to, or choose to disconnect from, will be a significant factor in the level of peace you can achieve.

- **Principle 3: Demand Your Worth** — The third chapter discussed understanding your *worth*, and how it can only be taken from you with your permission. Once you know it, you must protect it. The distinctions between status and worth were laid out. Chasing (and achieving) peace is possible, while chasing perfection is not. We talked about clarifying the concept of success and dropping comparisons, as well as magnetizing abundance by "being the magnet." Understanding you've had worth since birth will guide you back toward peace.

PROTECT YOUR MIND

- **Principle 4: Trust Your Vision** — The fourth chapter discussed homing in on your *vision* and then protecting it at all costs. We talked about using your own "lenses" vs. borrowing others, while not trying to convince anyone else of your vision. I introduced the "too-close bias" and urged you to become your own hero. Finally, we talked about being a finisher. Protecting your vision, while striving toward it, will open the door to peace.

- **Principle 5: Guard Your Focus** — The fifth chapter involved understanding how your *focus* is within your locus of control. We talked about rewiring what you focus on (disabling distractions) so that you are gripping the wheel of life, rather than idling in neutral. We discussed the importance of presence and "looking up." We reflected on receiving the baton in the race of life while preparing to pass it to the next in line.

- **Principle 6: Shift Your Perspective** — The sixth chapter talked about the significance of your *perspective*. We discussed the power perspective vs. the prison perspective—where does your perspective lie? I went over the intimate moments that ultimately led to one of the greatest shifts in my life. Another theme was the power in taking ownership over your life, as well as the commonality of negative thoughts and how everyone shares them. We discussed how to be "the Disruptor" in your life. We also talked about non-negotiables.

PROTECT YOUR SOUL

- **Principle 7: Simplify Happiness** — The seventh chapter dove in on simplifying *happiness*. As you work toward happiness and fulfillment, I recommend you include each of these four pillars in each day: intentionality, creativity, mobility, and spirituality.

- **Principle 8: Align Internally** — The eighth chapter was all about rewiring our tendency to align externally—and how becoming aligned internally is the ultimate game-changer. We discussed the power of betting on yourself. I provided various strategies to help you disconnect from external alignment and connect to internal alignment—and reap the harvest of your life.

- **Principle 9: Live in Fulfillment** — The ninth chapter wrapped up the soul section by discussing *fulfillment*. This chapter discussed the power of prioritizing life choices. We took a deeper dive into my most difficult seasons to date, and the shift into clarity that occurred as a result of my acceptance and my continuous healing. Last, I offered a few more reflections and insights on the meaning of *enough*, as well as how that relates to fulfillment.

LET GO OF THE GOAL

What I want to talk about now is falling in love with the *journey* instead of the *destination* in life. I understand this concept isn't groundbreaking, but let's get into why it's important. Destinations are something I have recently decided to let go of. In this next chapter of my life, I am falling in love, all over again, with my pursuit, without any specific destinations in mind. Destinations will come and go, but my pursuit will remain my focus.

You may be thinking, *In the personal development field, it's all about goals and destinations. How are you letting go of that, Trent?* Here's how. Goals and destinations are great, but sometimes we reach a goal and then we chill for wayyy too long. We stop being hungry and put our greatness on the back burner once again.

Here's what I want you to do: Use your vision to strengthen your daily process to keep you focused on your own pursuit. Refer to the daily necessities we discussed in Principle 7 to help you. Remix them to your own style, so that you develop a positive, healthy routine that you can stick to with consistency. Once you figure out how to sharpen your sword and do the small things for yourself every day that push you forward, you will start attracting rather than chasing. You'll start to become *the magnet.*

If you are the type of person who really thrives when you can focus on a goal or destination, start creating daily goals and destinations that you can check in on each night. Let's keep it simple: *Did I show up today? Did I live in purpose? Did I keep my commitments?* If the answer to these questions is yes, you won that day. If you start doing that every day, you are winning in life.

Shifting your focus from the destination to the pursuit will help keep you grounded in the present, but there are other benefits as well. You could end up heading in directions you might not have even dreamed of yet. And if you get too focused on a particular destination, you might be setting limits on how far you can really go. So many people make this mistake and create ceilings on their dreams that shouldn't exist.

I've met a lot of people who are just looking for momentary motivation. But I'm talking about turning this all into a lifestyle, piece by piece. Or, peace by peace, if you will. (Ha!) One piece at a time to improve on. Go slowly; you don't want to overwhelm yourself so that you quit the new lifestyle after a few weeks. Eventually, your life will improve as a whole, and you will be connected to your peace every day, regardless of what comes your way.

BUILT FOR IT!

Most great things in life are achieved in the face of resistance. Use the resistance to fuel yourself and understand, that when you are growing, you will often

THERE IS A REASON YOU HAVEN'T GIVEN UP. YOU ARE BUILT FOR THIS!

experience resistance before achieving desired results. Think about lifting weights: Resistance builds strength. Think about geology: Extreme pressure causes diamonds to form. Embrace the resistance.

In Principle 6, we discussed how we have all dealt with prison perspectives in our lives. Maybe you're dealing with that right now, thinking about what is working against you and always seeing the odds stacked against you. I want to shift that perspective, and what better place than to shift it than to your power! I understand the odds may be stacked against you, but I want you to appreciate the power we can bring to our lives when we overcome those odds. I don't care who or what is *against you*. I care about who and what is *for you*. My life changed when I made that shift for myself.

I know it's hard. I know you are stressed out. But you haven't quit and you are here! That tells me you are built for it. You are built for obstacles. You are built for losses. You are built for trials. You are built for struggles. You are built to beat the odds. You are built by the greatest to be the greatest! There is a reason you haven't given up yet.

Sometimes the reasons for it all aren't clear. Sometimes you don't understand. I get it. Sometimes you aren't meant to understand. But everything is building you. That person who walked out of your life? That's building you. The business that didn't go as planned? It's building you. Dealing with depression, anxiety, and loss? I know it's hard, but it's building you.

The mindset that sees the possibility and opportunity in everything is the mindset that is open to transformation. Approach everything with curiosity, even the unfavorable moments. What are they going to teach you?

Pause now and think about it. Scan back over your life. I'll bet it was the toughest moments that built your strongest faith. Those moments tested you, built your strength, and can serve as a reminder of all you're capable of! You know you are going to get through each season because you've already been through it.

When I start to feel pressure, I remind myself that I am built for this, and the reason I am in a good position is because of all the work I put in leading up to this moment. I acknowledge my pursuit will carry me through the pressure. I put in the work. I am meant for this moment and that is why I was called upon!

Now I feel lucky to experience pressure—purposeful pressure, that is. Being a father. Providing for my family. Building a business that can create generational growth. Speaking in front of thousands. There were times where each one of those roles would have been at the top of my list of what terrifies me. I reflect on what this pressure is going to teach me when it presents itself. Sometimes this comes in hindsight, but the more I get into my healing and growth, the quicker I can see which stressful seasons in life are going to teach me. I've started looking at these seasons as opportunities to grow and expand. Whatever tried to break me became what built me. When you develop this mindset, you become unstoppable.

A lot of us are trying to be perfect, but perfectionism brings the wrong kind of pressure. It's unnecessary pressure, and it leads to worry, guilt, and disappointment. When we have purposeful pressure and then add unnecessary pressure on top of it, we get overwhelmed and we miss out on the lessons the purposeful pressure is trying to teach us. Give yourself permission to be progressive rather than perfect. Take a step back and figure out how to separate the pressure you're putting on yourself from the pressure that's a natural part of the process.

You are built for this! I know sometimes you feel like you're not. The struggle makes it hard. Makes us lose sight. It's the tough moments that remind us to get back to who we are and what we are meant to do. You are uniquely suited to handle the adversities that arise in your life, and everyone one of them can teach you something. Yes, you're going to falter. Yes, things will get out of whack from time to time. That doesn't mean you can't get right again, like you have done over and over, ever since you took your first steps and busted your behind, only to get up stronger each time.

In this next chapter in your life, you will be walking in what I call "humble confidence." Not being full of yourself, but *loving* yourself fully. That's what we need in this world—me, you, and everyone else. So I need you to let go of thinking that your circumstances are unfavorable. Instead, understand that you are highly favored. Understand that *you can't lose.*

Saying it one more time for the people in the back: YOU ARE BUILT FOR IT! Do you hear me? You are built for what you are going through. You may have forgotten that. You may have forgotten who you are. It's time to remind yourself once again. Your next chapter will be your greatest yet. Everything you're going through will soon turn into everything you made it through.

It all starts with you. Let's get it!

Protect Your Peace Practice

You made it!

You made it! My greatest hope is that after your journey through this book, you feel more peace than you ever have. If that hasn't happened yet, apply what you have digested throughout this journey and your peace will begin to grow, my friend!

Don't forget about the mantra I want you to take with you. Repeat it out loud, or silently within your mind, whenever you need it:

I am Peace
I am Love
I am Healing
I am Free
I am Me!

I love you, my friend. You are meant to have peace and protect it. Don't forget that you are built for it!

YOU'RE A CHOICE AWAY FROM A NEW BEGINNING AND A COMMITMENT AWAY FROM A NEW LIFE!

LET'S GET IT

For more inspiration on your journey of protecting your peace, visit me at www.trentshelton.com. And keep on doing the Protect Your Peace Practices! Post your responses on your socials, as well as any other insights that hit home with you, and tag me **@TrentShelton** so we can continue to connect.

ENDNOTES

1. "Suicide Statistics [from the Centers for Disease Control and Prevention Data & Statistics Fatal Injury Report for 2021]," American Foundation for Suicide Prevention, accessed June 30, 2023, https://afsp.org/suicide-statistics.

2. Andree Hartanto et al., "Does Social Media Use Increase Depressive Symptoms? A Reverse Causation Perspective," *Frontiers in Psychiatry* 12 (March 2021). https://doi.org/10.3389/fpsyt.2021.641934.

3. J. Haidt and N. Allen, "Scrutinizing the Effects of Digital Technology on Mental Health," *Nature* 578 (2020): 226–7. https://doi.org/10.1038/d41586-020-00296-x.

4. E. J. Ivie et al., "A Meta-analysis of the Association between Adolescent Social Media Use and Depressive Symptoms," *Journal of Affective Disorders* 275 (2020): 165–74. https://doi.org/10.1016/j.jad.2020.06.014.

ABOUT THE AUTHOR

The number one mindset specialist and self-worth mentor in the world. One of the most impactful speakers of this generation. **Trent Shelton** reaches over 60 million people weekly through "real motivation" videos and unprecedented engagement. Trent connects with people all over the globe through his speaking engagements, podcast, books, mindset courses, and social sites. Trent is a motivational speaker who connects people to their purpose, their power, and their peace. It is his life's mission to connect people to the greatest version of themselves by communicating from his heart to yours. Trent is dedicated to showing the world that becoming your best self is possible and that it is your responsibility to make the world respect your greatness. It all starts with you. Let's get it.

Website: **TrentShelton.com**

Hay House Titles of Related Interest

YOU CAN HEAL YOUR LIFE, the movie,
starring Louise Hay & Friends
(available as an online streaming video)
www.hayhouse.com/louise-movie

THE SHIFT, the movie,
starring Dr. Wayne W. Dyer
(available as an online streaming video)
www.hayhouse.com/the-shift-movie

***

BE SEEN: Find Your Voice. Build Your Brand.
Live Your Dream, by Jen Gottlieb

THE HIGH 5 HABIT: Take Control of Your Life
with One Simple Habit, by Mel Robbins

THE GREATNESS MINDSET: Unlock the Power of Your Mind
and Live Your Best Life Today, by Lewis Howes

THE MOTIVATION MANIFESTO: 9 Declarations to Claim Your
Personal Power, by Brendon Burchard

All of the above are available at your local bookstore,
or may be ordered by contacting Hay House (see next page).

***

We hope you enjoyed this Hay House book. If you'd like to receive our online catalog featuring additional information on Hay House books and products, or if you'd like to find out more about the Hay Foundation, please contact:

Hay House, Inc., P.O. Box 5100, Carlsbad, CA 92018-5100
(760) 431-7695 or (800) 654-5126
(760) 431-6948 (fax) or (800) 650-5115 (fax)
www.hayhouse.com® • www.hayfoundation.org

———

Published in Australia by: Hay House Australia Pty. Ltd.,
18/36 Ralph St., Alexandria NSW 2015
Phone: 612-9669-4299 • *Fax:* 612-9669-4144
www.hayhouse.com.au

Published in the United Kingdom by: Hay House UK, Ltd.,
The Sixth Floor, Watson House, 54 Baker Street, London W1U 7BU
Phone: +44 (0)20 3927 7290 • *Fax:* +44 (0)20 3927 7291
www.hayhouse.co.uk

Published in India by: Hay House Publishers India,
Muskaan Complex, Plot No. 3, B-2, Vasant Kunj, New Delhi 110 070
Phone: 91-11-4176-1620 • *Fax:* 91-11-4176-1630
www.hayhouse.co.in

———

Access New Knowledge.
Anytime. Anywhere.

Learn and evolve at your own pace
with the world's leading experts.

www.hayhouseU.com